THE BOUNDARY BOSS WORKBOOK

ALSO BY TERRI COLE

Boundary Boss: The Essential Guide to Talk True, Be Seen, and (Finally) Live Free

THE
BOUNDARY
BOSS
WORKBOOK

THE RIGHT WORDS AND STRATEGIES TO FREE YOURSELF FROM BURNOUT, EXHAUSTION, AND OVER-GIVING

TERRI COLE, MSW, LCSW

sounds true
BOULDER, COLORADO

Sounds True
Boulder, CO

Sounds True is a trademark of Sounds True, Inc.

This book is not intended as a substitute for the medical recommendations of physicians,
mental health professionals, or other health-care providers. Rather, it is intended to offer
information to help the reader cooperate with physicians, mental health professionals,
and health-care providers in a mutual quest for optimal well-being. We advise readers to
carefully review and understand the ideas presented and to seek the advice of a qualified
professional if needed.

Published 2023

Cover design by Charli Barnes

Book design by Constance Poole

Printed in the United States of America

BK06735

ISBN: 978-1-64963-142-8

Ebook ISBN: 978-1-64963-143-5

10 9 8 7 6 5 4 3 2 1

Contents

Dear Reader

I'm curious . . .

When you know you need to set a limit or say no to someone, do you labor over the words and *still* end up feeling like it came out all wrong?

When you wait too long to draw a boundary or tell someone you have a problem with them, does it ever come out like an explosion rather than a calm and simple statement?

Do you avoid asking for what you want or speaking up about your preference because you just don't have the words and can't deal with the drama?

Would you like to free yourself from exhaustion, burnout, and over-giving and find peace, be able to assert your boundaries with ease, and live your life on your own terms?

If so, you're in the right place! Whether you've read *Boundary Boss* or not, *The Boundary Boss Workbook* is your roadmap to an entirely new way of interacting in your life!

What's a Boundary Boss? Simply put, a Boundary Boss is a person who is fluent in the language of boundaries. This means possessing the skills and words to communicate honestly, precisely, and with ease.

Think of boundaries as your own personal rules of engagement. They are guidelines you set in order to let others know what is okay and not okay with you. I define boundaries as knowing your preferences, desires, limits, and deal breakers, and having the ability to communicate them when you so choose. It's telling the truth about how you feel and about what you DO and DO NOT want and need.

Bad boundaries are exhausting, whether they are too rigid or too porous; whether you're unyielding or a pushover. Neither is a good way to go through life. If you have rigid boundaries and someone does something you don't like, you might ghost them or withdraw in anger. If you have loose or nonexistent boundaries, you're doing *all the things* for *all* the people *all* the freakin' time. Either way, you end up feeling frustrated, angry, and alone. You feel used and abused without realizing you're serving yourself up on a silver platter by doing things for others that they can and should be doing for themselves.

Not being fluent in the language of boundaries is not your fault. You've likely observed and internalized disordered boundaries as the norm since birth. Disordered boundaries are unconscious behavior patterns that have been ingrained in us since very early childhood. Most of us were raised and praised to be self-abandoning codependents. It's no wonder we have issues with boundaries. How often did we hear "Be good," "Turn that frown upside down," or "If you don't have something nice to say, don't say anything at all"?

Many of us were conditioned to be outwardly focused on the wants, desires, needs, and comfort of other people. We learned to do whatever we needed to avoid negative feedback from the grown-ups in our life. We may struggle with disappointing others or saying no because we're still driven by a childhood fear of rejection and judgment. First, it came from our parental impactors, and then the behavior was reinforced by our teachers, friends, bosses, and coworkers. And it doesn't stop there, the message is repeated in TV and movies, on social media, and in every corner of our society. Over and over we're told that being kind, generous, nice, and self-sacrificing is desirable, and having strong boundaries makes us self-absorbed, dramatic, or mean.

The solution is simple. It's not easy, but it *is* simple. When you know your preferences, desires, limits, and deal breakers, you don't spend your life catering to or blaming other people. You're able to kindly and gently let people know how you feel, what you're willing to do, and what your boundaries are. Learning to regularly establish healthy boundaries on your own is like trying to speak a language nobody taught you. But just like a language, with the proper information and instruction, you can learn it.

WHY ARE BAD BOUNDARIES SUCH A PROBLEM?

In my experience, I can say with certainty that unhealthy boundaries are the number one cause of pain and suffering for my clients and can readily doom relationships to fail. People caught in unhealthy boundary patterns live on a sort of hamster wheel of frustration, bitterness, and anger. They feel like others are taking advantage of them and don't know how to make it stop. The resentment accumulates over time as they don't express their needs or set limits.

If you've read the *Boundary Boss* book, you know what a boundary disaster I was. There was no request I wouldn't say yes to. No over-functioning I couldn't handle. Seriously, in my twenties, I was a bridesmaid eight times! I was frustrated, resentful, and most of all, exhausted.

The good news is I was able to turn all that around by learning how to speak a new language. I literally changed the words that came out of my mouth and changed my life.

I've also seen the same boundary issues in thousands of clients. Best of all, I've been able to help those clients rewire their behavioral patterns and change their lives.

After writing *Boundary Boss*, I was asked repeatedly for more exercises, more scripts, and more ways for readers to help themselves become more empowered in their relationships. They wanted more ways to practice because *knowing* how to set healthy boundaries is not the same as *doing it*. And although practice does not "make perfect" per se (because we're humans) it sure does elevate your boundary-setting capabilities. This workbook is going to raise your awareness to the blocks you may be experiencing, give you the emotional tools you need to succeed, and teach you to write clear, concise boundary scripts.

You'll make small yet powerful changes that will lead to breakthroughs in your relationships because *everything* changes when you do!

WHAT WILL HAPPEN WHEN YOU IMPROVE YOUR BOUNDARY SKILLS?

Proactive boundary skills can empower you to eliminate the cycle of frustration or emotional pain in relationships. Our conditioned patterns and behaviors are automatic responses. It's like you're going through life on autopilot without any thought to the fact that you have a choice in the matter.

Interrupting the automatic response, even for just a few seconds, allows you to stop and think. Do you *really* want to say yes to a request to host a twenty-person holiday meal on your own? Or would you prefer to switch it to a potluck and share the prep work? Are you *really* okay with the fact that your sister borrowed money and has not paid it back yet? Or are you frustrated and having a conversation about a payment timeline would help?

The self-care, self-soothing, meditation, breathing, and self-reflection techniques you're going to learn are about slowing down to give you two to three seconds of delayed response time in every interaction. That's all it takes to stop, see the choice, and make a more empowered decision. (Again, simple but not necessarily *easy*.)

People think boundaries are all about the other person's behavior, but really, it's about yours. Once you start setting boundaries, you change. You become more assertive. You understand what you want. You get to know yourself. Your confidence and self-esteem will start to rise. You get to be your authentic self. And most of all, you realize how you feel, what you think, and what you want, matters.

HOW LONG WILL IT TAKE TO BECOME A BOUNDARY BOSS?

People always want to know how long it's going to take to change their lives. All this newfound satisfaction with life sounds great and all, but I have things to do! Listen, it took your whole life to build these disordered boundary patterns, and they're not going to just disappear overnight. Becoming a Boundary Boss is a lifelong practice. You'll find that even small changes in your communication will have a huge impact on your well-being. Once you start to notice changes happening in your life, my hunch is that you'll want to keep going and the exercises, mindfulness practices, and strategies in this book are here to support you.

The way we create a new normal is through repetition. And there will always be new levels of boundary conversations to navigate. You'll start with setting boundaries in low-risk situations like sending back the salad that is not the one you ordered. Then you'll move up to family and friend situations that might feel a little more high-risk. Over time, the fear subsides little by little, and the next thing you know, you're handling work negotiations with your boss with ease and confidence.

Ultimately, that's what having healthy boundaries is all about—the ability to advocate for your preferences, needs, limits, and deal breakers—while respecting the boundaries of others at the same time. People tell me all the time that it was worth the effort and time they put in because they found such peace and satisfaction on the other side of creating their own healthy boundaries.

SETTING BOUNDARIES IS LOVING, NOT SELFISH

Boundaries are compassionate and loving. They help us build strong relationships in all areas of our lives because they teach people how to treat us. When you leave things unspoken, you're setting yourself up to feel disappointed and frustrated when people don't meet your expectations. No one can read your mind, and it's not fair to expect them to. If you really want something from someone in a relationship, you can't leave it unexpressed. You need to actually use words to succinctly communicate your preferences and desires.

Showing other people the real you, expressing your needs, and being truly yourself sets you free. And it sets everyone else free, too. When you can be appropriately vulnerable and share your true feelings, you're creating an authentic connection with another. You might be surprised how many people will say, "Thank you so much for your candor." You may be surprised at how many people will actually validate you: "I didn't realize how much I interrupted while you were talking. Thank you so much for telling me. I will work to be a better listener." Or even "You're right, the amount of work you do around here does deserve a raise."

If you care deeply about the relationships in your life, be assured that setting boundaries is only going to make them stronger. We're so conditioned to complain about reason number 1,042 why Bob's a jerk and file the resentment away in our heads. But it's so much braver to simply talk to Bob and tell him that his comments made you feel unappreciated. Maybe he has no idea he was being insensitive and apologizes. Great! You can move on with your day. But even if he doesn't apologize, you can feel good about standing up for yourself and making an empowered choice to be seen.

Setting boundaries is not a lever of control to pull in order to get your way. It's not about manipulation. It's about knowing your preferences, your desires, your limits, your deal breakers, and having the ability to communicate them.

Having healthy boundaries is your right but it's also your obligation if you want to have healthy relationships. It's not about anyone else; it's about you. By the end of this workbook, you'll have the tools and strategies to effectively communicate your desired boundary requests. Most importantly, you'll have the skills to do it *your way*. There's no one-size-fits-all when it comes to expressing your boundaries. It's what's right for you.

HOW TO USE THIS WORKBOOK

The Boundary Boss Workbook is set up in three sections: Get Ready, Get Set, and Go! These sections will take you on a journey from self-awareness to self-mastery, and the best part? You get to keep your new skills for life. I've designed these exercises to be simple and doable so that you can work through them right inside the pages of this book. Or if you love journaling, you can also do the exercises in your own separate journal. Here's what you'll find in each section:

Get Ready: We'll start by looking inward and raising your awareness by defining boundaries and the most common boundary blocks you may be experiencing right now. You'll also identify your personal preferences, desires, limits, and deal breakers which are your unique building blocks to healthy boundaries.

Get Set: Next, you'll get prepared for what could go right and what feels like could go very wrong as you practice boundary setting. The activities in this section are going to help rewire your nervous system to be less reactive to the fear of rejection, judgment, and shame. Instead, you'll learn to respond as someone who knows that boundary setting is about protecting yourself, your integrity, and your relationships.

Go: Alright, you're ready for the big time—taking your new skills out into the world and using them with the relationships in your everyday life. You're going to learn how to set healthy boundaries by creating scripts that follow your own natural style. You'll be able to hold your ground in a kind way, using words that feel comfortable and natural to you.

In the back of the book, you will find additional boundary script writing resources that include how to buy time instead of giving an insta-yes, additional script starters, how to say no with ease, and a section on techniques to make your boundary scripts even more successful.

Throughout the workbook I've built in mini-breaks to reinforce what you are learning:

Say It With Me 💬 are positive affirmations to empower

Do It With Me 🙌 are quick, powerful actions for you to take to stay on track

Loving Reminder 🖤 are loving little truth bombs from my heart to yours

All the exercises build on each other, so don't skip around. Even if you read *Boundary Boss* cover to cover and feel like you've improved your boundary setting skillset, you're in a different place now—so your answers and approach will be different. There are growth opportunities at every level of our Boundary Boss journey!

What you feel and what you want *matters*. In fact, they matter the most! It's time to give the people in your life the opportunity to show you how much you matter as well. It's going to take some work, but that's okay. You're not that fragile. And your relationships are not that fragile either. You can handle it.

I've taught thousands of people just like you how to create and sustain lives that they absolutely love based on self-knowledge, self-compassion, self-love, and my proven techniques for transformation.

Your potential for true happiness is my driving force in all of the work that I do, and I am deeply committed to adding value to the quality of your life. I know this workbook will do just that.

Let's do this!

BOUNDARY BASELINE ASSESSMENT

The questions in this brief assessment are designed to clearly establish your current *Boundary Baseline*. Think of it as a snapshot of your boundary-setting skillset. You've got to understand where you are right now before you can begin to make any lasting changes!

Please take ten minutes to answer these eighteen short questions. The more thoughtful and honest you are in your answers, the more helpful and illuminating your results will be.

➔ *If you had to choose just one, which best describes your boundary status right now?*

☐ I'm boundary curious and ready to learn more.

☐ I have okay boundaries and I want to improve.

☐ My boundaries are solid in some relationships, weak in others, and I could use help.

☐ I'm a boundary disaster and I feel stuck.

☐ Other _____

➔ *Why do you want to develop the ability to draw healthy boundaries? (Check all that apply.)*

☐ Speak my truth   ☐ Less conflicts

☐ More joy and harmony   ☐ Better relationships

☐ Uplevel my professional life   ☐ More freedom

☐ Self-protection   ☐ Other _____

→ *What stops you from drawing boundaries? (Check all that apply.)*

☐ Not sure how   ☐ Fear of punishment

☐ Anxiety   ☐ Other _____

☐ Guilt   ☐ Other _____

→ *Do you think people will view you as mean, selfish, rude, or offensive if you draw boundaries or speak up?*

☐ Yes   ☐ No

→ *Do you already know what boundaries are and the importance of them?*

☐ Yes   ☐ No

→ *Does the thought of drawing boundaries create anxiety for you?*

☐ Yes   ☐ No

→ *How difficult do you find it to draw boundaries right now? On a scale from 1 to 5, with 1 being easy and 5 being very difficult*

[1]   [2]   [3]   [4]   [5]

easiest   *very difficult*

→ *Do you use passive-aggressive communication to express your opinions when boundaries are being violated?*

☐ Yes   ☐ No

→ *Can you connect your current anger, resentment, anxiety, fear, and/or frustration to boundary violations?*

☐ Yes   ☐ No

➔ *Do the conflicts in your life originate from the lack of clear, concise boundaries? (Or the violation of these?)*

☐ Yes   ☐ No

➔ *Who are the people you find it most difficult to draw boundaries with? (Check all that apply.)*

☐ Spouse / Partner   ☐ Friends

☐ Children   ☐ Frenemies

☐ Parents   ☐ Boss

☐ Siblings   ☐ Coworkers

☐ Other relatives   ☐ Other _____

☐ Lover / Date   ☐ Other _____

➔ *Did you have good role model(s) for healthy boundaries growing up?*

☐ Yes   ☐ No

➔ *Do you know what your preferences, desires, limits, and deal breakers are?*

☐ Yes   ☐ No

➜ *List two to three of your biggest challenges with boundaries today.*

_____

_____

_____

_____

_____

_____

_____

➜ *What is your intention and desire for your Boundary Boss Workbook experience? What results would you like to achieve?*

_____

_____

_____

_____

_____

_____

_____

_____

_____

_____

_____

_____

_____

_____

No matter what your assessment reveals, please come to this journey with gentle curiosity since *The Boundary Boss Workbook* is strictly a NO JUDGMENT ZONE. ;) We will revisit these questions and answers at the end of the workbook so you can gauge just how far you've come!

Loving Reminder 🖤

Your past behavior is not a reflection of
who you are, just what you knew at the time.

PART 1

Get Ready

Welcome to your Get Ready portion of *The Boundary Boss Workbook*.

In this section we begin our Boundary Boss journey by looking inward and raising your awareness about what boundaries actually are, and the most common boundary blocks you may be experiencing right now. You'll also begin to identify your personal preferences, desires, limits, and deal breakers.

Self-awareness is the first step to advanced growth and sustainable transformation. It is important to get honest about what is and is not working in all areas of your life because what you're tolerating may be getting in the way of your ability to create healthy boundaries. The information you glean from these exercises will be used later in this workbook as a GPS to which relationships and situations need your attention. The more you understand why you relate to boundaries the way you do, the easier it becomes to shift your behavior from unempowered to self-determined!

As you experience the awareness-raising phase of our boundary-building adventure please luxuriate in this opportunity to simply explore your true feelings. Consider this time of self-reflection as a gift most people rarely give themselves. Go, YOU!

COMMON STRUGGLES TO SETTING BOUNDARIES

For many, the inability to say no, set limits, or assert their honest preferences is perceived as a fatal personal flaw. It's easy to label yourself *weak, stupid,* or just a *pushover.* (Fill in your own self-blaming adjective.) But these labels are not the truth. What I have found over my years of teaching this content is that they simply weren't taught to us. If you struggle with knowing and expressing your preferences, limits, and deal breakers . . . there is nothing wrong with you. Becoming fluent in the language of boundaries is the same as learning any language—it takes a great teacher and some practice.

➔ *Review the list below and check off the ones that are true for you.*

☐ No one ever taught you about boundaries

☐ Fear of rejection

☐ You have the *disease to please*

☐ Not having discernment (like where a boundary is needed)

☐ You struggle with codependency

☐ You don't know where to start

☐ You are conflict avoidant

☐ Ineffective communication

☐ In denial that you need them

☐ Not realizing when a boundary has been crossed

☐ You don't know the right words to use

☐ You worry what others will think of you

☐ You are afraid of hurting someone's feelings

☐ You don't know your preferences, limits, and deal breakers

If you checked one or all of the boxes, you are in good company. The good news is that with practice and time, anyone can learn to successfully overcome these obstacles and that includes you!

➜ *From your checked boxes, choose two or three that you struggle with the most. Below or on a separate piece of paper, journal to reflect on why.*

_____

_____

_____

_____

_____

_____

_____

Do It With Me 🙌

Stand up and give yourself
a full-body stretch.

HEALTHY BOUNDARIES

Sometimes the word boundary can be misleading because the connotation can feel negative, like forcefully shutting down situations or other people. Boundaries are so much more than being able to say no to others. It might surprise you to learn that, in fact, healthy boundaries actually open doors, hearts, and opportunities. Healthy boundaries help us to protect our time, energy, space, material, and mental resources. This liberates us to show up more fully in our lives, careers, and relationships.

➔ *Review the list below and check off the ones that you would like more of in your life.*

- ☐ To confidently say yes or no when you want to
- ☐ Separate your needs, thoughts, feelings, and issues from others
- ☐ Prioritize your own preferences & pleasures
- ☐ Build high self-respect leading to more self-esteem
- ☐ Express compassion without taking on the feelings of others
- ☐ Create relationships with equitable power & responsibility
- ☐ Accept no from others
- ☐ Share personal information gradually, in a mutually sharing and trusting relationship
- ☐ Protect your physical and emotional space from offenses, intrusion, and violations
- ☐ Feel more secure, centered, and protected
- ☐ Have the ability to end unhealthy relationships
- ☐ Manage your time well
- ☐ Rest or take a nap when you are tired
- ☐ Not working on your days off

➡ *From your checked boxes, identify your top two or three, or add your own. Use the space below to expand. Why do you want it? What positive changes might happen as a result?*

_____

_____

_____

_____

_____

_____

_____

_____

_____

Say It With Me 💬

I have the right to say no (or yes) to others
without feeling guilty.

PERSONAL BOUNDARIES

Do you struggle to assert your boundaries or feel confused about what boundaries you might be lacking? In this exercise I'm breaking down different types of boundaries and how to identify boundary violations, PLUS giving you some tips and scripts so you will have the words you need to assert healthy boundaries. Your boundaries are as unique as you are. Clearly communicating your boundary preferences, limits, and deal breakers are like sharing your own Rules of Engagement with others. It transparently identifies permissible ways for others to interact with you and sets relationships up to succeed.

The following is a breakdown of the different categories of boundaries you can use to build your personal Rules of Engagement.

Physical Boundaries

Your most basic physical boundary is your body. Physical boundaries include who has the right to touch you and how much personal space you need. Physical boundary violations include someone grabbing you without your permission or barging into the bathroom without knocking. Asserting a healthy physical boundary can sound like:

> "I'd like to make a simple request that you knock before you come into my room."

> "Please take a step back. You are standing too close for my comfort."

➜ *Who are you comfortable being touched by (partner, friends, family, coworkers, etc.)?*

_____

_____

_____

➜ *How are you comfortable being touched by others? (Do you prefer a fist bump to a hug?)*

_____

_____

_____

Sexual Boundaries

Sexual boundaries are commonly considered a subset of physical boundaries. You alone get to decide what sexual touch is acceptable. How, when, and with whom you have intimate exchanges must be self-determined.

Someone coercing, pressuring, or forcing you to be sexual with them without your expressed consent are examples of sexual boundary violations. This can include someone massaging your shoulders, sexual comments, or jokes that make you feel uncomfortable. Asserting a healthy sexual boundary could sound like:

"I don't appreciate sexual jokes or comments, please don't say things like that around me."

"Do you have a condom? I don't have unprotected sex."

"Sending unsolicited sexual images or messages is not okay with me, please don't do it."

→ *Do you know your personal values, beliefs, and boundaries when it comes to sexual behavior and relationships? Please expand:*

_____

_____

_____

_____

→ *Do you feel comfortable saying "no" to unwanted physical or sexual behavior? Please expand:*

_____

_____

_____

_____

Material Boundaries

Material boundaries represent the ways you relate to your material possessions and how you want other people to relate to them. All of the conditions and stipulations around your "stuff" are in this category. A material boundary violation would be someone using your computer without asking or borrowing clothes out of your closet without your permission. Asserting your material boundary around money lending might sound like:

> "I have a 'no lending' money policy. So, it's not personal, but the answer will have to be no."

→ *How many people have access to the things you own? Please expand:*

_____

_____

_____

→ *Do you lend money or not? Please expand:*

_____

_____

_____

_____

➜ *Are there any areas of your home that are off-limits to others? Please expand:*

_____

_____

_____

_____

_____

Mental Boundaries

Mental boundaries are about your values, opinions, and beliefs. Healthy mental boundaries mean you know what you believe and what you think about things. It also includes the ability to listen to others, even when you don't agree with them. Having healthy mental boundaries allows you to take in what someone else is saying, even if it's a difficult conversation, without shutting down or exploding. It is holding onto your own opinion, even if you are in the minority. Violation of your mental boundaries looks like someone disparaging your beliefs or making demands instead of requests. Do you have someone in your life who often tries to wear down your no? This looks like you expressing your boundary and clearly saying no, and the other person guilting you, making you wrong, or trying to convince you to change your mind. (So exhausting!) To assert a limit, you might say:

"You've asked and I've answered."

"We will have to agree to disagree because I won't tolerate you belittling my opinion."

➜ *What signifies to you that it's time to walk away from a discussion? (Is a friendly debate okay but not a heated one? Learning to opt out before you reach your limit is an important skill to have!) Please expand:*

_____

_____

_____

_____

_____

➜ *How well do you interact with someone whose beliefs you disagree with? Can you listen with a desire to understand rather than be right? Please expand:*

_____

_____

_____

_____

_____

Emotional Boundaries

You are responsible for your feelings just as others are responsible for their feelings. Having healthy emotional boundaries means you are clear about what is on your side of the street, so to speak, and what isn't. You don't blame others for the way you feel and you don't accept blame for how someone else feels. If you have weak emotional boundaries, you might feel compelled to "fix" things for the people around you or give unsolicited advice or spontaneous criticism.

You might get very emotional, combative, or defensive regularly. An example of an emotional boundary violation is someone telling you, "You shouldn't feel that way." No one has the right to tell you what you should or shouldn't feel. Asserting an emotional boundary sounds like:

> "I'm sharing my feelings with you, not asking for your opinion or your approval for my feelings."

→ *Who are you comfortable being vulnerable about personal situations with?*

_____

_____

_____

_____

_____

_____

➔ *What types of information are you uncomfortable sharing with friends, family, etc.?*

_____

_____

_____

_____

_____

_____

_____

_____

Loving Reminder

Healthy boundaries can
spare you years of bullshit.

Healthy Boundaries Matching

➔ *Draw a line to match the boundary type to the corresponding healthy boundary:*

BOUNDARY TYPE	HEALTHY BOUNDARY
1. Physical	**A.** Agreeing to disagree (and not discuss politics) with loved ones who hold different beliefs than you.
2. Sexual	**B.** Granting your partner's request for an hour of alone time to cool off after an argument.
3. Material	**C.** Someone asking if they may hug you or if you are more of a hand shaker.
4. Mental	**D.** Requesting that others remove their shoes as they enter your home.
5. Emotional	**E.** Sharing your sexual preferences with your partner.

KEY: 1C, 2E, 3D, 4A, 5B

Boundary Offenses Matching

➜ *Draw a line to match the boundary type to the corresponding boundary offense:*

BOUNDARY TYPE	BOUNDARY OFFENSE
1. Physical	**A.** Someone saying, "You have no reason to feel that way."
2. Sexual	**B.** Someone massaging your shoulders without your consent.
3. Material	**C.** Someone saying, "I can't believe you are stupid enough to vote for ____. He is an idiot."
4. Mental	**D.** Someone borrowing your stuff (clothes, tools, car, laptop, etc) without your permission.
5. Emotional	**E.** Someone pressuring you to have sex after you have clearly stated you are not ready.

KEY: 1B, 2E, 3D, 4C, 5A

BOUNDARY TYPES

Within each category of personal boundaries, there are three types: rigid, porous, and healthy. If yours are too loose or too tight, that's often symptomatic of boundary issues. A common misconception is that having strict boundaries is equivalent to having healthy boundaries. Not so. Being inflexible actually gets in the way of building healthy relationships in the same way that being too flexible does.

RIGID:	HEALTHY:	POROUS:
• not ask for help when you need it • avoid close relationships to minimize rejection, perceived by others as detached or cold • tend to isolate yourself • when offended or hurt, you're more likely to cut someone off than share vulnerable feelings	• value your own thoughts and opinions • feel comfortable asking for or accepting help • know when to share personal information and with whom • can accept and respect the boundaries of others, including someone saying no to a request	• overshare your personal information • say yes when you want to say no • find yourself taking on or overly investing in the problems of others • put up with disrespectful or abusive behavior

➡ *Pick two or three of the boundary type characteristics that resonate most to expand upon below or in your journal.*

_____

_____

_____

_____

_____

_____

_____

_____

_____

_____

_____

_____

If you have healthy boundaries, you know when certain boundaries are appropriate. What's appropriate with family and friends may not be with coworkers or your boss. Context matters. For example, if you had a painful breakup, sharing your heartache with your besties is appropriate. Sharing the details of your breakup with a subordinate or your boss is not. Healthy boundaries guide you to be appropriately self-contained or vulnerable depending on what the situation calls for. And remember: building the skills to regularly establish and enforce healthy boundaries is a process!

POROUS & RIGID BOUNDARIES PRACTICE

Personal boundaries are you deciding what types of communication, behavior, and interaction are acceptable to you. If you never learned how to establish healthy boundaries, trying to figure out how to set them can be challenging. If your boundaries are too lax or porous, you end up allowing other people's boundaries to dictate what happens to you.

On the other hand, having overly-rigid boundaries creates its own set of problems with intolerance and control. No matter where you fall on the boundary spectrum, awareness is the first step to establishing, changing, and enforcing healthy boundaries.

It is not uncommon to have one style of boundaries at work and another with your family or partner. Our goal is the same regardless, which is to systematically transform the majority of our boundary interactions into healthy interactions.

Check your knowledge of porous and rigid boundaries by completing the exercise on the following page.

Take the Boundary Style Quiz!
A quick, 13-step quiz designed to identify your boundary style & how it can be improved!
Go to boundarybossworkbook.com/extras

➔ *Review the statements and put an R next to the description of rigid boundaries (too firm) and a P next to the descriptions of porous boundaries (too loose).*

	P / R	BOUNDARY STATEMENT
1.		I can be easily frustrated if others don't view things the same way that I do.
2.		I find myself saying yes when I really want to say no to avoid conflict.
3.		I am out of touch with my own feelings and rarely share how I feel with others.
4.		Emotionally I keep most people at a distance.
5.		I find myself making excuses for the bad behavior of others towards me.
6.		I find myself doing more than my share of participating in the relationship.
7.		I often use anger and/or intimidation to get others to do what I want.
8.		I tend to try to "fix" other people and their problems.
9.		I put the needs and wants of others before my own.
10.		I can be critical of others when they don't do things the "right way" (which happens to be my way!).

KEY: 1, 3, 4, 7, 10 are rigid
2, 5, 6, 8, 9, are porous

WHAT EXACTLY ARE YOU TOLERATING?

As humans, we have learned how to tolerate a lot. We tend to take on, accept, deal with, and get weighed down by other people's situations, behavior, unfulfilled needs, boundary violations, frustrations, issues, and even our own self-sabotaging behavior. And although you might make it look easy . . . it takes a toll.

You are likely tolerating more than you may realize. So, let me ask you directly, what are you tolerating? Please take a moment to list below at least ten things (situations, circumstances, people, feelings) you sense that you are tolerating in your life right now. Examples:

My lack of self-love, unbalanced workload at home, self-medicating because I am so overwhelmed, feeling invisible, etc.

KNOW YOURSELF TO KNOW YOUR BOUNDARIES

The foundation of creating healthy boundaries is self-knowledge and self-understanding.

This is why it is so important to make the distinction for yourself about what is simply a preference, what is worth negotiating for, and what is a nonnegotiable deal breaker.

- A preference is *nice to have* but not crucial. For example, you may prefer coffee over tea or a bath over a shower.
- A limit may be that you are no longer willing to, for example, lend a sibling money or do more than your share of the household chores.
- Deal breakers are your nonnegotiable boundaries. For example, you may have a zero-tolerance policy for abusive language or phones at the dinner table.

Knowing what is and isn't okay with you (and to what degree) will help you make decisions that are rooted in your truth. Take this opportunity to create your personal list of preferences, limits, and deal breakers for each life domain. In your journal or on a separate piece of paper, explore the circumstances, relationships, and feelings in all areas of your life. The more you understand yourself, the easier it will be for you to identify and construct your desired boundaries in all areas of your life. Here are some prompts to guide you.

Personal Space	How much do you require? Do you prefer a handshake or a hug? Do you like to be touched or not? How does it differ when it is close friends, coworkers, family, a lover, a stranger, and acquaintances?
Work	Is the work that you're doing working for you? How do you interact with coworkers, the environment, working conditions, culture, and physical environment?

Finances	What is okay with you regarding your finances, spending, saving, sharing a budget with a partner, or splitting expenses with others? Is it okay if you have a small savings or do you need to have a lot in the bank to feel okay?
Love & Dating	Is being in a relationship or casually dating your preference? What is your favored form of communication (text, phone calls)? How do you like to problem solve? How much time together or apart is okay with you in a relationship? What, where, when, and with whom is sex okay?
Body	Is your physical health and wellness okay where it is right now? If you are physically able, do you have daily or weekly habits that are nonnegotiable (movement, yoga, meditation, etc.)? Do you want to consistently have healthier habits but fail to follow through?
Home	How do you prefer your surroundings to be? Noise level, lighting, vibe, textures, cleanliness?
Beliefs & Opinions	Are you okay with other people's beliefs and opinions if you don't agree? Can you listen with an open mind, or do you become judgmental? Can you stand behind your own beliefs or opinions if someone else disapproves? Is it okay with you to have a spirited debate or not?
Your Stuff	Is it okay for others to borrow your possessions, eat food off of your plate, or borrow money?
Communication	Do you like a lot of communication with friends, family, and partners, or not? Deep dive or keep it light? Phone, in person, texts, or handwritten letters? Is it okay if people interrupt while you're talking?
Social	Do you prefer going out or staying in? Are group activities okay or do you prefer more one-on-one time? Live music, parades, parties, bars, crowds, okay or not okay?
Relationships	List anything that is currently happening in any of your relationships that is not okay.

KNOW YOUR BOUNDARY RIGHTS!

So much of the work of creating an empowered life is understanding and claiming your boundary rights, so let's go!

The Boundary Boss Bill of Rights

1. You have the right to say no (or yes) to others without feeling guilty.

2. You have the right to make mistakes, to course correct, or to change your mind.

3. You have the right to negotiate for your preferences, desires, and needs.

4. You have the right to express and honor all of your feelings if you so choose.

5. You have the right to voice your opinion even if others disagree.

6. You have the right to be treated with respect, consideration, and care.

7. You have the right to determine who has the privilege of being in your life.

8. You have the right to communicate your boundaries, limits, and deal breakers.

9. You have the right to prioritize your self-care without feeling selfish.

10. You have the right to talk true, be seen, and live free.

 Get the Boundary Boss Bill of Rights for your phone or refrigerator. Go to boundarybossworkbook.com/extras

Your Turn

→ Read the Boundary Boss Bill of Rights **out loud**, replacing the "You" with "I."

→ Which of the Boundary Rights do you currently struggle with?

_____

_____

→ Did any of the rights on this list surprise you or not occur to you?

_____

_____

→ Write three new Boundary Rights you would like to add for yourself.

1. _____

2. _____

3. _____

Do It With Me 🙌

Place one hand on your belly, the other on your heart and breathe deeply for 60 seconds.

SIGNS A BOUNDARY HAS BEEN CROSSED A.K.A. BOUNDARY OFFENSES

Your body is constantly sending you signals. Whether it is a gut feeling, heart racing, or even a headache, your body's reactions hold the answers to your mind's questions. This exercise focuses on how your body alerts you when someone crosses your boundaries. Being socialized to second-guess our lived experiences and feelings is more the rule than the exception. The more you understand and honor the gems of wisdom from your brilliant body, the easier it will be to know where you need to establish a boundary by setting a limit or making your preferences clearly known.

POSSIBLE SIGNS A BOUNDARY HAS BEEN CROSSED	
Physical sensations, such as:	*Emotional sensations, such as:*
• Constriction in your chest	• Feeling resentment
• Pain in the throat	• Feeling irritated or annoyed
• Freezing up	• A desire to flee
• Muscles tense	• Something feeling "off"
• Gut or head pain	• Sudden anger or frustration
• Accelerated heartbeat	• Feeling burned out

Your body always knows. If you are unsure if a boundary has been crossed, do a body scan. Then, check your resentment. If you feel resentful about it, it can be a red flag that a boundary has been crossed or a need is not being met.

→ *Take a moment and think about these boundary-crossing examples:*

- The moment someone makes a rude or offensive comment.

- You've already clearly said no, and someone asks you the same thing again.

- When someone goes into your phone and reads your text messages without your knowledge or consent.

- When someone is twenty minutes late to dinner again with no notice.

What's the response in your body? Is there a constriction or a tightness? It could be in your chest, your stomach, or your throat. Does your head start to hurt or do your cheeks flush? You might even physically cringe away from someone. You might go into a fight, flight, freeze, or fawn reaction.

_____

_____

_____

_____

_____

_____

_____

INSTA-YES

Automatically saying yes is a common boundary problem and can be the result of lifelong conditioning. Often, we simply do what other people want us to do as a way of being nice, helpful, or loving without thinking about the long-term consequences. It is also not appropriate or authentic for us to say yes to everyone who asks. Anything automatic is a reaction, not a mindful choice and you don't owe anyone a definite yes or an immediate response. In this exercise, we are raising your awareness of when and under what circumstances you give an insta-yes (or even a maybe) when your gut says no.

Think about the last time you automatically said yes and use the prompts below to deepen your self-understanding. Repeat anytime you find yourself giving an insta-yes.

→ *Who did I say yes to when I wanted to or should have said no?*

_____

→ *What was the circumstance?*

_____

→ *I gave an immediate yes because I was afraid that:*

_____

_____

→ *I gave an immediate yes because I was worried that if I said no:*

_____

_____

ARE YOU OVER-FUNCTIONING?

Over-functioning refers to doing more than is required, expected, or appropriate and being unclear about what IS your responsibility and what's NOT. Have you ever been in a relationship (romantic or platonic) where you regularly did more than your share of the work and the other person did less (under-functioned)? Or maybe it started out more balanced and then developed into an over/under-functioning dynamic?

This behavior dynamic is exhausting and the first step to changing it is to recognize it. Review the over-functioning characteristics below and put a check next to the ones that sound like you. Once you know where you are doing it, you can begin to make small changes to put appropriate boundaries in place.

☐ Being overly focused on *actively* solving another person's problem.

☐ Frequently giving unsolicited advice.

☐ Doing things that are part of another person's responsibilities.

☐ Feeling like if you don't get it done, (even if it's not yours to do), no one will!

☐ Feeling exhausted from doing too much.

☐ Feeling underappreciated and resentful from doing too much.

☐ The thought of stopping over-functioning for loved ones creates anxiety and a sense of being out of control.

→ *How is the over/under-functioning dynamic familiar to you? Did you witness this dynamic growing up? Please expand.*

_____

_____

_____

_____

_____

_____

_____

Bring one relationship to mind and answer the questions.

➔ *Name the individual for whom you over-function:*

_____

➔ *Name exactly what you do that is not your responsibility:*

_____

_____

_____

_____

_____

_____

➜ *Name what you think or fear would happen if you suddenly stopped:*

_____

_____

_____

_____

_____

➜ *Make a list of actions and behaviors that you now recognize as over-functioning that you can eventually work toward stopping:*

_____

_____

_____

_____

_____

_____

YOUR VIP SECTION

Imagine that your life has a VIP section like a club. You are in charge of that area, you create the guest list, and you are the only bouncer. This exercise is to help you make a distinction between nonpriority people who feel entitled to take a VIP seat in your life, and your real-deal priority peeps who belong there. Not everyone deserves a twenty-four-hour backstage pass to your amazing life. YOU get to make that choice.

Your VIPs don't have to be perfect. They're human, like you, but they certainly should not leave you feeling constantly drained, used, or abused. Whether relatives, friends, or demanding colleagues, you don't need to dramatically excommunicate anyone, unless you want to. You can create healthier boundaries that limit others' access to you. Part of the Boundary Boss journey means shifting away from the mindset of the conditioned self and moving toward a conscious, self-determined life!

Now it's time to make your VIP list. Bring one relationship at a time to mind. Based on the answers to the questions below, place that person in the correct column.

Use the following questions to help you determine where to place them. Does spending time with this person energize or deplete you? Do you look forward to spending time with them or secretly kind of dread it? Does this relationship feel like an obligation rather than a choice? Is the relationship based on the other person's desire to spend time with you rather than your own?

VIP	NON-VIP WHO FEELS ENTITLED	NON-VIP WHO YOU TREAT AS VIP

WHO ASKED YOU? (AUTO-ADVICE GIVING)

When someone is talking about a problem they're having, do you feel immediately compelled to give your thoughts, opinions, previous experience, or knowledge to help FIX their problem?

Compulsive auto-advice giving is a form of "unhealthy helping." It is a learned dysfunctional boundary behavior and a codependent tendency that ultimately blocks or limits intimacy in relationships. This behavior can be well-intentioned, but it can also be intrusive and frustrating for the receiver.

➔ *Think about a recent conversation you had and make a list of any unsolicited advice or criticism you gave OR received and how you felt.*

_____

_____

_____

_____

_____

Say It With Me 💬
I have the right to determine who has
the privilege of being in my life.

MAKING ASSUMPTIONS

A common relationship pitfall is making assumptions. Leaving things unspoken sets you up to feel disappointed and frustrated when people don't meet your expectations. If you really want something from someone in a relationship, you can't leave it unexpressed. You need to communicate your desires openly and honestly because no one can read your mind, and it's not fair to expect them to. Expressed agreements are vital to every relationship, whether it's with your coworker, client, your best friend, family members, or your romantic partner.

➔ *To see where you might be making assumptions, consider these questions and check off yes or no.*

YES	NO	
		Do you assume that others know how you're feeling or what you're thinking without you having to tell them?
		Do you assume the other person has the same morals, values, and integrity as you without having a conversation to find out?
		Do you assume that the other person remembers details or events that you consider important, without verifying that they do?
		Do you ever think, "I shouldn't have to tell her that," or "he should know that by now?"
		Do you assume that the other person will react the same way you would in a given situation?

➔ *Take a moment to write down some examples of when you've made assumptions past and present. You can use the prompts as a guide.*

- Who does it happen with?
- What is the situation?
- How does it make you feel?

_____

_____

_____

_____

_____

_____

_____

_____

Loving Reminder 🖤

It's not your job to convince anyone of your
right to have healthy boundaries.

LIES WE TELL

Taking an inventory of where you might be making excuses to avoid a conflict or have to establish a boundary will help you gain a deeper understanding of your behavior.

Think about it like this: you are unconsciously distorting the facts or rationalizing the behavior of others so that you won't have to have a conversation that may feel too threatening to you.

Examples:

"I know my partner didn't intentionally forget our anniversary, they have a lot on their plate right now."

"I'm sure my friend didn't mean to exclude me from their plans, they were probably just forgetful."

"I'm sure my coworker didn't mean to miss the deadline, they must have been dealing with something personal."

"I'm afraid if I go to Human Resources about Betty's behavior I will be labeled as a drama queen or a troublemaker."

"My partner often loses their temper with me. I know it's because they suffered abuse growing up, so I don't say anything because I don't want to make them feel bad."

➜ *Bring to mind some interaction you had that left you feeling frustrated, angry, or upset, then use the prompts to ask yourself:*

- Who was involved?
- What was the excuse or lie you told yourself?

_____

_____

_____

_____

_____

_____

_____

_____

Say It With Me 💬

I have the right to voice my opinion
even if others disagree.

RECIPROCAL BOUNDARIES

When we talk about boundaries, it's most often from the perspective of how to set and maintain our own personal boundaries. The truth is, being a Boundary Boss also means you have the ability to respect and accept other people's boundaries as well.

An example of respecting others' boundaries is if your best friend requests that you do not give unsolicited dating advice, and you listen to her without resentment and refrain from giving advice. We need to give others respect and autonomy to make their own decisions. Each of us has a right to sovereignty and to be self-directed in our choices.

The Boundary Boss Bill of Rights for Other People:

1. Other people have the right to say no (or yes) to me without feeling guilty.

2. The people in my life have the right to make mistakes, to course correct, or to change their minds.

3. Everyone has the right to negotiate for their preferences, desires, and needs.

4. Everyone has the right to express and honor all of their feelings if they so choose.

5. Other people have the right to voice their opinion even if I disagree.

6. Everyone has the right to be treated with respect, consideration, and care.

7. Everyone has the right to determine who has the privilege of being in their life.

8. The people in my life have the right to communicate their boundaries, limits, and deal breakers.

9. Everyone has the right to prioritize their self-care without feeling selfish.

10. Everyone has the right to talk true, be seen, and live free.

→ *Which of the rights do you struggle with as they relate to others? Choose your top two or three and journal about them below.*

_____

_____

_____

_____

_____

_____

_____

_____

_____

_____

Do It With Me 🙌

Write down 3 things you're grateful for.

BOUNDARY AWARENESS RAISING TRACKER

This tracker will help keep your healthy boundary behaviors in your conscious mind. Fill it out now and see if you can challenge yourself to use it every day this week. The more mindful you are, the more proactive you can be, and the more you will strengthen your boundary muscles. I can't wait to see what you find out about yourself. Reliable data is the queen of sustainable transformation! If you love this, you can download it at boundarybossworkbook.com/extras.

MY DAILY BOUNDARY AWARENESS RAISING TRACKER	
Boundaries I need to initiate	Boundaries I need to enforce
Boundaries I need to respect	Emotional check-in *In one word, how am I feeling right now?* *(Take care to name your feeling accurately.)*

Check off each time you do any of the following.

M T W Th F S Su

☐ ☐ ☐ ☐ ☐ ☐ ☐ Gave an insta-yes

☐ ☐ ☐ ☐ ☐ ☐ ☐ Gave auto-advice

☐ ☐ ☐ ☐ ☐ ☐ ☐ Over-gave

☐ ☐ ☐ ☐ ☐ ☐ ☐ Made an assumption

☐ ☐ ☐ ☐ ☐ ☐ ☐ Didn't respect someone's boundary

☐ ☐ ☐ ☐ ☐ ☐ ☐ Made an excuse for someone else

☐ ☐ ☐ ☐ ☐ ☐ ☐ Gave a nonpriority person VIP treatment

REFLECT

This brings us to the end of our Get Ready section of the workbook! Please take some time to reflect on what you learned in this awareness-raising phase of your Boundary Boss journey.

➔ *What were your biggest Aha Moments?*

_____

_____

_____

_____

_____

➔ *What were your biggest breakthroughs?*

_____

_____

_____

_____

_____

_____

_____

_____

➜ *What questions did the exercises and activities in this section bring up for you?*

_____

_____

_____

_____

_____

Say It With Me 🗩

I have the right to negotiate for my
preferences, desires, and needs.

PART 2

Get Set

Welcome to your Get Set portion of *The Boundary Boss Workbook*.

In this section, you will be continuing your Boundary Boss growth journey and transitioning from raising awareness to acquiring real self-knowledge. You are also entering what I call *the in-between*. This is the phase where you now know enough not to automatically engage in the old behaviors but have not yet mastered the new ones. And, you're on your way! The in-between is a powerful part of the journey. You're learning new skills and behaviors and on your way to mastery.

The mindfulness practices in this section will support you to be more present while changing your boundary patterns. Self-care is a foundation for your success. If you're feeling fear, anxiety, or guilt, cut yourself some slack. It's normal to feel these emotions when we start to transform the boundary dances in your relationships. You got this! (And I got you ♥.)

BOUNDARY MYTHS & TRUTHS

Do you ever worry about how you will be perceived if you speak up, express a limit, disagree, or simply say no? Many people fear being misunderstood or negatively labeled with phrases, such as *drama queen, difficult, high maintenance, hysterical, moody, hormonal, mean, or selfish*. Society has taught us to value being agreeable and above all, **nice**. And saying no or stating our actual preferences can feel like we're being self-absorbed, controlling, or bitchy. Let's check out the top boundary myths that might be keeping you stuck in an old familiar boundary pattern.

Boundary Myth: Boundaries will alienate the people I love.

Boundary Truth: Healthy boundaries serve to protect your relationships so they can thrive.

Boundary Myth: Real romantic love needs no boundaries.

Boundary Truth: Healthy love ALWAYS requires healthy boundaries.

Boundary Myth: Protecting my boundaries makes me selfish.

Boundary Truth: Protecting your boundaries makes you brave & generous.

Boundary Myth: Creating healthy boundaries is too time-consuming.

Boundary Truth: You could spend the rest of this lifetime (and the next) cleaning up the mess that past unhealthy boundary disasters created.

Boundary Myth: Setting boundaries makes me mean.

Boundary Truth: Setting boundaries can consistently be done with kindness.

Did you notice that the boundary myths are all driven by fear-based thinking? So why is it so scary to assert healthy boundaries? It all comes back to fear of rejection, abandonment, or conflict. But rest assured that none of those experiences is fatal and the more you can exercise expressing your preferences, desires, limits, and deal breakers, i.e., healthy boundaries, the more you will reap the rewards and the less threatening it will feel.

→ *Take a moment to journal about the boundary myths from above that trip you up the most, and why. Are the myths related to messaging from your family of origin or the culture you grew up in?*

_____

_____

_____

_____

_____

_____

_____

_____

Loving Reminder

Asking for what you prefer does not mean
you are criticizing someone else.

MISNAMING YOUR EMOTIONS

Shifting toward better boundaries means understanding what you're feeling and what you need so you can communicate clearly. One of the most powerful tools in building better emotional regulation is simply identifying and naming the emotion you are feeling.

Misnaming emotions is a common phenomenon. To be understood by others we need to first understand our own emotions. Instead of using broad definitions like "bad or good"—ask yourself, were you feeling sad, hopeless, ashamed, or anxious? I have found having a list of more nuanced emotions is helpful in this process. Getting in touch with your feelings, frustrations, and emotions creates the opportunity to clearly understand precisely what you need, leading to transparent boundary requests.

➔ *List ten different emotions you have felt recently. Be specific instead of using broad definitions like "bad" or "good"—were you feeling sad, hopeless, ashamed, anxious, or something else?*

1. _____

2. _____

3. _____

4. _____

5. _____

6. _____

7. _____

8. _____

9. _____

10. _____

→ *Do you allow yourself to feel a full range of emotions or do you stifle some?*
Please expand.

_____

_____

_____

_____

_____

_____

_____

_____

_____

Get an in-depth emotions list at
boundarybossworkbook.com/extras

THE ART OF NOT TAKING THINGS PERSONALLY

This exercise will help you to start to filter your experiences and raise your awareness about where you might be taking things personally. Not taking things personally is easier said than done *and* it's a process. It is empowering to learn how to come from a place where what's happening externally isn't always about you. Remember, reality is ALWAYS subjective and the only reality you can be responsible for managing is your own. It might be hard to believe, but other people's behavior toward you is not personal. What they are doing is about *them*, and how you react or respond is about *you*.

When you are in the in-between phase of becoming fluent in boundaries and feeling anxious about changing your boundary interactions, you may do one or more of the following:

Assign Meaning

We are wired to make meaning. It's part of the human experience. However, it is essential to be aware that you might be making up stories or scripts to fill in the blanks of why someone did or said something when, in reality, you don't really know!

Make Assumptions

This one goes hand-in-hand with assigning meaning. This is about being mindful and staying on your side of the street. It's about not assuming you know the personal motivations of others . . . because, truly, unless you ASK, you don't!

Catastrophize

Catastrophizing, sometimes referred to as fortune telling, is to imagine the worst possible outcome of a situation or event. Beginning the process of setting boundaries, especially in established or difficult relationships, can feel threatening and your fear-based thinking can conjure up the worst-case scenario as a way to dissuade you from speaking up or setting a limit.

Project

Projection is a psychological defense mechanism, unconsciously employed to protect us from pain or discomfort. Projection happens when we disavow feelings that are uncomfortable or out of alignment with how we see ourselves and we reassign those feelings to someone else.

→ *Looking at the list above, where do you see yourself and your reactions to others? Choose those that resonate with you the most and journal about when you do it, with whom, and why?*

_____

_____

_____

_____

_____

_____

_____

_____

IF I WERE BRAVE

This exercise will help you gain clarity on what you really desire and give you the opportunity to flex your courage muscles. The goal is to remove ingrained or unconscious blocks or limitations. Often, we are operating within negative assumptions about ourselves, our abilities, and our potential. This exercise gives you the freedom to try on a feeling state (like being brave) without the threat of having to take any immediate action. Approach it like a fun game. Allow yourself to get expansive, use your imagination, and tap into your truest heart's desires.

We'll look at the nine main areas of your life: In each area, all you have to do is finish the sentence, "If I were brave, I would . . ." For example, in the area of health and romantic relationships, you might write:

If I were brave, I would . . .

FITNESS AND HEALTH	ROMANTIC RELATIONSHIPS
. . . Sign up for the yoga training course I have been thinking about starting for two years. . . . Make an appointment for a physical. . . . Start to drink 64 oz of water a day.	. . . Invite my partner to read the new erotica book I brought with me. . . . Tell the person I am dating we are not a match.

→ *Now fill in your own statements. "If I were brave, I would . . ."*

Family of Origin	Family Life	Friendships and Social Events
Work and Career	Creative Projects	Fitness and Health
Finances	Romantic Relationships	Your Home

Once you have completed your lists, sit with them for a while. Visualize the feeling of taking action on your brave lists. Don't put pressure on yourself to do anything immediately—simply visualize and feel the feelings of having those things become your reality.

HOW IS YOUR SELF-CARE?

How do you think your life might change if your needs, desires, and well-being commanded as much consideration as everyone else's in your life? I can tell you from experience that prioritizing self-care in small ways on a daily basis will positively impact every aspect of your life. Many of us were raised to believe that self-care is *selfish*. This is simply untrue. In fact, a lack of self-care is one of the hallmarks of disordered boundaries and codependency. We can be so busy making sure everyone else is taken care of that our own self-care never materializes. The truth is, self-care is a crucial component of becoming a Boundary Boss.

It's time for a quick self-care inventory. Answer the questions below to get a snapshot of where your self-care is right now, and whether you need to make any adjustments. (I'm going to guess you do 😊.)

→ *What part of your mental, physical, or emotional health needs your attention? For example, what might need to change in the areas of sleep, physical wellness, nutrition, hydration, downtime, meditation, self-reflection, your financial life, etc.?*

_____

_____

_____

_____

_____

_____

➜ *Can you identify any specific people or experiences that seem to spark bad habits?*

_____

_____

_____

_____

_____

_____

_____

Take a moment to reflect on what you learned about your current level of self-care. Don't worry if you need a little inspiration and guidance—flip to page 72 for 30 mindfulness and self-care ideas! You got this . . . and I got you 💕.

Say It With Me 💬

I have the right to prioritize my
self-care without feeling selfish.

SELF-SOOTHING TOOLKIT

Regularly practicing self-soothing is a game-changer when it comes to wrangling the stressful feeling of being *in-between* your old boundary dances and establishing your new ones. During any times of change, emotions can run high. This can be exacerbated if you already have anxiety challenges or are feeling overwhelmed by the stress and unpredictability of the world. Learning to self-soothe can help to regulate your emotions, inspiring a more calm and centered state. When we're in the grips of setting boundaries and emotional overload it can be difficult to remember the things that work to soothe us.

I suggest creating this toolkit in advance so it's available to help you in the moments when you need it. You can put the items in a pretty box or silk bag, or put a few in your purse for a self-soothing toolkit on the go.

➜ *Take some time and find out what you find calming. Jot down a few items for each category:*

TOUCH	SOUND
Tactile fabric, stones, small stuffed animal.	**Soothing music, voice, talk to someone.**
1. _____	1. _____
2. _____	2. _____
3. _____	3. _____

SIGHT

Favorite pictures of
people, places, or things;
meaningful quotes
or poems.

1. _____

2. _____

3. _____

TASTE

Something small—Hershey's
Kisses or other chocolate, a small
bag of something crunchy,
Tic Tacs or mints.

1. _____

2. _____

3. _____

SMELL

Candle, essential oils, or even small amounts of spices
you have in your kitchen like rosemary, cinnamon, peppermint.

1. _____

2. _____

3. _____

30 DAYS OF MINDFULNESS & SELF-CARE

Think of ways of taking care of yourself that are outside the box of what you normally do because most of the time, most of us are prioritizing the crap out of other people in our life to the detriment of ourselves. Time for that to change!

Below are 30 mindfulness and self-care activities to inspire you. Pick one to do each day of the month and cross it off as you go. Let's GO!

Start your day with a short guided meditation.	Do an activity your inner child would love, like going on a swing.	Spend time in nature, such as going for a walk or sitting in a park.
Take a moment to think of someone you are grateful for, and silently send them well wishes.	Imagine a soothing scene, such as a peaceful beach or a forest, and take a few moments to visualize yourself in that place.	Write a thank-you note to a friend who did something nice for you and tell them or send it to them.
Stretch for five minutes.	Take a dance break.	Take a nap.
Prepare one of your favorite foods.	Do something simply because it is fun.	Read a book or your favorite magazine.
Unplug and go screen-free for at least an hour.	Spend time with people who light you up!	Dress up or down today for no reason.

Treat yourself to a small indulgence, such as your favorite dessert or a new book.	Remove any equipment or appliances that make you feel bad.	Spend an hour alone (or as much time as you can).
Go outside and breathe deeply for four minutes.	Have a date night with yourself.	Sing a favorite song out loud for no reason.
Write down three things that bring you joy.	Create a music playlist with five or more of your favorite tunes.	Take a moment to appreciate something in your surroundings, such as a plant or a piece of art.
Take a relaxing bath or shower.	Gently stretch your body.	Write an affirmation on your bathroom mirror.
Repeat a word or phrase that has special meaning to you.	Color a picture or make a doodle on a piece of paper.	Place your hand on your heart and focus on the sensation of your heart beating.

 Scan to get my self-love guided meditation

INTERNAL BOUNDARIES

Internal boundaries are the boundaries you set within yourself. They represent effective management of your thoughts, emotions, time, and behavior. They directly reflect the health of your relationship with yourself. Disordered internal boundaries might show up as procrastination, not following through on your word to yourself or others, an excess of negative self-talk, and not taking good physical, emotional, spiritual, or mental care of yourself.

When you have healthy internal boundaries, you can consistently rely on yourself to do what you say you're going to do. Choosing not to abandon yourself (or damage your relationships) not only strengthens your internal boundaries but also builds your self-esteem.

➔ *Check the boxes that apply to you:*

☐ Are you frequently plagued with feelings of guilt, remorse, or worry that you said or did the wrong thing in a given situation?

☐ Do you have a loud "inner mean voice" endlessly making negative comments and assessments of you?

☐ Do you find it difficult to tap into your intuition?

☐ Do you make excuses for yourself?

☐ Do you use language that is inaccurate? Do you say ten minutes but mean an hour?

☐ Do you overpromise?

☐ Do you proclaim you will change unhealthy habits and fail to follow through?

☐ Are you easily swayed by someone else's opinions, thoughts, judgments, or criticism?

☐ Are you indecisive?

☐ Do you set goals only to abandon them within a few weeks?

☐ Is it difficult for you to speak your truth if you know others will disapprove?

➜ *To amplify your self-awareness, please choose three to four of the above statements that you said yes to and journal about them using the following prompts:*

- Why do you think it's true?
- How does it make you feel?
- Did you see this behavior modeled?
- How do you want it to be?

_____

_____

_____

_____

_____

_____

Do It With Me 🙌

Drink a big glass of water. (For a treat add
oranges, cucumbers, or lemons!)

HOW YOU TALK TO YOURSELF

People look to you to set the example of what you believe is acceptable behavior. Who you draw into your life and how they treat you is influenced by how you treat and regard yourself. If you are your own worst critic or feel unworthy, you will inevitably draw people into your life who will agree with your self-assessment. On the other hand, if you treat yourself with respect and love, and hold yourself in high regard, most others will follow your lead.

→ *Journal below about your inner dialogue and the specific negative things you say to yourself when you're frustrated, angry, or down.*

_____

_____

_____

_____

_____

_____

_____

_____

_____

➜ *Ask yourself the following questions and journal your answers below.*

- Would a good friend say or think this about me?
- What would a loving pal say about me instead?
- What would I say to a friend who thought this about themself?

_____

_____

_____

_____

_____

_____

_____

_____

_____

_____

LITTLE YOU

In this exercise we are focusing on attending to the child within. To keep "little you" in the front of your mind, please choose a baby picture from under the age of eight years old. This picture can become your screen saver, or you can print it out and put it on your fridge or in a frame where you will see it often.

Below you will find an agreement to make with yourself:

I Promise Myself. . . .

To face this work and any challenges I may encounter, with the support and encouragement of unconditional self-compassion. I will speak to myself, treat myself, and envision myself with love, support, and encouragement. I will pay attention to my needs and do my best to address those needs with love, understanding, and action. I make this pledge to myself because I know unconditional self-compassion and prioritizing my preferences and pleasure can be difficult to sustain during times of growth and transformation. I am committed to the well-being of my inner child and the grown-up me and will act accordingly.

➔ *Now, write down all of the amazing, special, or sweet things about you as a little kid.*

_____

_____

_____

_____

_____

BOUNDARY AFFIRMATIONS

Whatever we set our attention on grows. Creating personalized affirmations that resonate with you is a powerful (and fun!) way to inspire transformation. When you notice negative self-talk or fear-based statements running through your mind, gently bring yourself back to your positive affirmation and feel the feelings associated with it. Be mindful of the fact that words have wings and creative power. They can take flight and set things in motion. Speak about yourself, your life, and your potential the way you want it to be.

I am worthy and deserving of setting and maintaining my boundaries.

Every day I'm more clear about the boundaries that best serve me.

I speak my truth with ease, grace, and courage.

I set boundaries with kindness and ease.

I speak my needs unapologetically.

➡ *Practice saying the affirmations above aloud and create a few for yourself.*

1. _____

2. _____

3. _____

Get a powerful boundary-affirmation tapping routine at boundarybossworkbook.com/extras

POST-BOUNDARY-SETTING ANXIETY

Setting new boundaries can kick up feelings of regret, anxiety, guilt, or fear. Having a desire to "take back" the boundary is a normal part of the transition to becoming a boundary master. Just because you feel guilty or fearful does not mean you have done something wrong. This is especially true if folks in your life are manipulative or experts at getting you to abandon your boundaries.

It takes time to transform self-abandoning behaviors, codependency, and over-functioning into better-boundaried interactions. Change can be scary, and anticipation of people's reactions can leave you reeling. If you can expect to be uncomfortable after setting a boundary, you will not be blindsided or sent into a panic when you feel post-boundary-setting anxiety. Learning to sit with your discomfort and not react too soon is essential to your boundary-setting success.

→ *What's your biggest fear when setting boundaries with others?*

_____

_____

_____

_____

_____

_____

_____

Below are a few strategies to keep in mind after initiating a boundary, especially if you're feeling anxious.

Time

You may have a desire to "undo" the boundary, but wait. Commit to not taking action for twenty-four to forty-eight hours. The more evidence you gather that drawing boundaries does not lead to something terrible, the easier the entire process gets, and the sooner you move through the fear brought on by the IN-BETWEEN.

Care

Every time you recognize that your mind is obsessing about what you fear the other person is thinking about you, STOP and bring your attention back to you. Take actions that soothe you. Move your body, spend time in nature or a calming space, meditate, watch a mindless movie, call a pal, snuggle a pet, take a bath, and just give yourself a break.

Patience

When you are feeling post-boundary-setting anxiety, think back to different successful boundaries you've drawn or shifts you've made. Try to remember how you felt then and how relieved and empowering it felt to stick to your boundary. People and relationships are usually much more resilient than we think.

Even when you become a true Boundary Boss, you may never love having the tough conversations. Time and repetition will continue to lessen your anxiety and taking the actions that you know are right for you will become your new normal.

REFLECT

This brings us to the end of our Get Set section of the workbook! Please take a few minutes to reflect on what you learned in this phase of your Boundary Boss journey.

➜ *What were your biggest Aha Moments?*

_____

_____

_____

_____

_____

➜ *What were your biggest breakthroughs?*

_____

_____

_____

_____

_____

→ *What questions did the exercises in this section bring up for you?*

_____

_____

_____

_____

_____

_____

_____

_____

_____

_____

Say It With Me 💬

I have the right to be treated with respect,
consideration, and care.

PART 3

Go

Welcome to your Go portion of *The Boundary Boss Workbook.*

In this section, you are continuing to build your Boundary Boss skills by crafting personalized boundary scripts to use in your everyday life. You'll learn to hold your ground, make simple requests, or say no (or yes) in a kind way, using words that feel comfortable and natural to you.

You'll also learn how to effectively and easily communicate your preferences, desires, limits, and deal breakers, which will positively impact all areas of your life.

APPROVE OF YOURSELF

This exercise can help you develop a greater sense of self-trust and self-confidence, and challenge the limiting belief that you need someone else's approval or permission to do what is important to you. By acknowledging that you don't need external validation, you can free yourself from the constraints of seeking approval from others and feel more empowered to take risks and pursue your dreams since it's your life, baby! For example, if the original statement was, "I can't start my own business because my family won't approve," the reframed statement might be, "I do not need approval from my family to start my own business."

➜ *Write down something that you have been holding back on or that you have been hesitant to do because you feel that you need someone else's approval.*

Next, reframe the statement using the phrase "I do not need approval to . . ."

SOMETHING YOU HAVE BEEN HOLDING BACK ON	I DO NOT NEED APPROVAL TO . . .
. . . I can't start my own business because my family won't approve.	. . . I do not need approval from my family to start my own business.

→ Now fill in your own statements and snap a picture as a reminder that you don't need to seek external validation or approval to live your life, your way.

I DO NOT NEED APPROVAL TO . . .	

Do It With Me 🙌
Crank up your fave dance tune and shake
what your mama gave you!

EFFECTIVE & INEFFECTIVE COMMUNICATION

There are only two types of communication: effective and ineffective. Effective communication is direct and to the point, leaving no doubt as to what you mean. You're assertive, but not aggressive or passive. Ineffective communication is not stating what you want in a manner that can actually be received by the other party. This usually makes others feel mystified, miffed, and misunderstood. Once you uncover how you've been communicating, you can start to take steps to improve. Effective communication is an essential component to creating clear, transparent boundaries which leads to having real, healthy relationships.

The goal of this exercise is to see what behaviors need your attention and intention to transform. And remember: effective communication is a requirement for becoming a Boundary Boss! Use what you learn as a place to start improving your communication style.

➜ *Read through the effective and ineffective communication traits. In each column, circle what resonates with your current communication style.*

➜ *Did you have more effective or ineffective communication traits?*

_____

_____

➜ *List 2-3 traits that you want to improve.*

_____

_____

_____

INEFFECTIVE	EFFECTIVE
Indirect: not getting to the point, never clearly stating intention	**Direct:** to the point, leaving no doubt as to meaning
Passive: timid, reserved	**Assertive:** not afraid to state what is wanted or why
Antagonistic: angry, aggressive, or hostile in tone	**Congenial:** affable and friendly
Cryptic: underlying message obscured, requiring interpretation	**Clear:** underlying issues are articulated
Hidden: true agenda never directly stated	**Open:** no intentionally hidden messages
Non-Verbal: communicated through body language and behaviors rather than words	**Verbal:** clear language used to express ideas
One-Way: more talking than listening	**Two-Way:** equal amounts of talking and listening
Unresponsive: little interest in the perspective or needs of the other person	**Responsive:** attention paid to the needs and perspective of the other person
Off-Base: responses and needs of the other person are misunderstood and misinterpreted	**Accurate:** responses and needs of the other person are understood and respected
Dishonest: false statements are substituted for true feelings, thoughts, and needs	**Honest:** true feelings, thoughts, and needs are stated

HOW ARE YOU COMMUNICATING?

No one's communication is 100-percent ineffective or effective. But just like figuring out how to bake a cheesecake, cite a research paper, or dance salsa, effective communication skills can be learned. You have the potential to be an expert communicator over time. The goal is progress, not perfection.

→ *Check yes or no for the questions below:*

	YES	NO
Do you often feel misunderstood?		
Do you feel frustrated on a regular basis?		
Do you communicate directly or do you hint and imply instead?		
Do you communicate directly or are you passive-aggressive in your communication?		
Do you minimize your own feelings by saying everything is okay or fine when you're actually angry?		
Do you withdraw in anger or give someone the silent treatment when you are upset?		
Do your words not match what's happening inside of you? (Like saying, "I said, I'M FINE!" when you do not feel fine.)		
Were you taught that being too honest is rude?		

→ *Choose two to three questions that you said yes to and go deeper. Below or in your journal, ask yourself: who is it with, who did you learn this behavior from, how does it make you feel, and how would you like to be able to respond instead?*

_____

_____

_____

_____

_____

_____

_____

_____

Loving Reminder

Celebrate each and every mindset shift,
no matter how big or small.

ASKING EXPANSIVE QUESTIONS

What is the antidote to auto-advice giving? Learning to pause and ask expansive questions instead of jumping in to fix or offer advice. The next time someone comes to you with a problem, instead of automatically giving them advice, try out one of these expansive questions:

What does your gut instinct say?

How do you feel about it?

What do you think you should do?

Then just be silent and wait. These kinds of questions are supportive without overstepping boundaries or compromising another's sovereignty. It may be hard to do this initially, but the more you practice, the easier it will get. Remember, the truth is you truly do not know what anyone else should do. What actually helps them the most is supporting them to come to answers on their own.

Now You Try

Practice what you would say below in the following situations.

Your friend shares with you that she is upset because her coworker Bob presented her idea as his own in their team meeting.

→ *Your response:*

_____

_____

_____

_____

_____

_____

Your friend shares with you that they gave their cousin a two-week loan and it has
been a month and the money has still not been re-paid.

→ *Your response:*

_____

_____

_____

_____

Do It With Me 🙌

Give yourself a 5-minute hand massage using
whatever lotion you have available.

EVALUATING SCRIPTS

When writing boundary scripts, the goal is to inform the other person of your preference, desire, request, or limit, and, in some cases, your deal breakers.

For example, you might say, "I'd like to make a simple request that when you borrow the car, you bring it back full instead of empty." Or "I wanted to bring it to your attention that your texting throughout our family meeting today was distracting to me. I'd like to request that at next week's meeting you abide by our agreed-upon rules and leave your phone in your room."

Avoid adding qualifying statements to your requests (e.g., "You'll probably think this is crazy, but . . ."). Also, reduce approval-seeking questions (e.g., "Does that make sense?" "Is that okay?"). It is not about seeking their approval of your choices, preferences, or desires but about being more accurately understood.

Example: Betty asked you to work for her next week, you originally said yes and now you need to let her know you can't. An appropriate script to let Betty know you can no longer work for her might sound like this:

> "Betty, a family obligation has come up and now I am sorry I am unable to work for you next Thursday. I reached out to Kevin to see if he can do it."

→ *In the scripts below, see if you can identify the missteps in the language (they can contain more than one):*

A. Too wordy

B. Unclear

C. Unnecessary explanation

D. Trying to convince

E. Justifying

F. Overly aggressive

G. Blaming

	SCRIPT
1.	Betty, I know I said that I could work for you next Thursday, but it turns out that an old friend of mine is coming into town and even though she told me she was coming I forgot to write it down. And I did ask her if I could do it on Friday night, but she has other plans. So now my working for you next Thursday is going to be a problem.
2.	Betty, I can't work for you next Thursday because when you asked me, I was doing something on my computer and was distracted. Next time, I hope you will learn to wait until I am not doing something else so this doesn't happen again.
3.	Betty, my friend got tickets to see Madonna next Thursday and I know I said I would work for you, but it really is the opportunity of a lifetime! If the tables were turned, I would understand if you wanted to go to a concert instead of work for me. I've been working so much lately that I really could use a break and you're the one who's always telling me to take care of myself.
4.	Betty, I changed my mind and can't work for you next Thursday. If you have a problem with that you can take it up with HR!

KEY 1 A and C, 2 G, 3 D and E, 4 F

BOUNDARY OFFENDERS

Do you know any Boundary Bullies, First-Timers, or Repeat Offenders? These are people who violate your boundaries with and without knowing they are doing it. From a friend who always manages to plan the meet-up near her apartment to a boss who ignores your requests to stop contacting you about work on the weekend. Interacting with them can be stressful and leave you feeling defeated and drained.

Whether you're dealing with a First-Timer, a Repeat Offender, or a Boundary Bully, your job is to stay dialed into your own feelings and goals. It is prudent to consider that Boundary First-Timers might be more clueless than malicious, which is why clearly pointing out a boundary offense or making a boundary request is a required part of boundary-setting success.

BOUNDARY FIRST-TIMERS	BOUNDARY REPEAT OFFENDERS	BOUNDARY BULLIES
People to whom you have never actually expressed a boundary request with words. (i.e., You have not yet given them a chance to change their behavior.)	People to whom you have stated your boundaries, and yet they continue to cross the line that you have explicitly drawn.	People who want what they want regardless of how you feel or how you approach them. They can act in overtly or covertly manipulative ways to get what they want from you.
When dealing with First-Timers, you need to clearly and calmly make a boundary request.	When dealing with Repeat Offenders, you need to get a verbal commitment and/or add specific consequences to your boundary requests.	When dealing with Boundary Bullies, if negotiating or adding consequences is not effective, you can proactively protect yourself by limiting their access to you.

Knowing who your biggest boundary offenders are and bringing mindful awareness to the issue when you're not in the heat of the moment is a great place to start building your boundary resilience and confidence.

➔ *Think about some recent interactions and make a list of who the Boundary First-Timers, Repeat Offenders, or Boundary Bullies are below:*

BOUNDARY FIRST-TIMERS	BOUNDARY REPEAT OFFENDERS	BOUNDARY BULLIES

Loving Reminder 🖤

Your thoughts matter. Your preferences matter. Your needs matter. Your boundaries matter because YOU matter!

STOP THE INSTA-YES

We often feel pressure to respond to others right away. In truth, you don't owe anyone an immediate response, so when someone asks something of you, take pause. If you can stop automatically saying yes to things that you really don't want to do, you are stopping the process and creating space to breathe. Below are some simple scripts to push pause on the insta-yes:

"Thank you, I'll have to check my calendar."

"I will need to sleep on that. For my sanity, I've implemented a twenty-four-hour decision-making policy."

"I want to check with my partner (or sister, roommate, friend, etc.) before committing."

"I will need to get back to you on that but thank you for thinking of me."

Consciously internalizing the truth that you don't owe anyone an instantaneous yes liberates you to do fewer things you don't want to do, which also lowers your level of resentment. It's a win/win! Understanding that you have a right to set boundaries and say no is key to being successful at this. Boundaries don't exist to punish other people, boundaries are to protect your energy, your health, your emotional safety, and your relationships. When you don't tell the truth about how you feel, you end up angry and resentful. Directly saying no and drawing a boundary isn't just protecting you, but it's also allowing people to know you.

Examples of how to say no:

"I can't make it on Wednesday but hope you have an amazing time!"

"I'm sorry. I don't have the bandwidth to help with your project right now."

"I have decided to keep my Sundays open for family/volunteer/solo time so I will have to say no but appreciate you thinking of me."

"Thank you for thinking of me but I won't be able to make the party."

"Gotta say NO to dinner at 11:00, but I'm always a YES to you, my friend. Let's have brunch next weekend."

The more honest you are about your preferences and limits, the less you will do a bunch of crap that you don't want to do, and the better your relationships and self-esteem will be.

→ *To help you get comfortable using new boundary language, practice saying the different boundary phrases in this exercise in the mirror. Then you can practice with a pal and start to employ your version of the phrases when needed, working from lower-priority people to higher-priority. The more you do it— the easier it becomes!*

Loving Reminder 🖤

Asking for help makes you brave, not weak.

TAKE A RESENTMENT INVENTORY

Taking an inventory of where you might be harboring resentment in your relationships can help provide a snapshot of where a need is not being met, a boundary needs to be established, or where a boundary has been violated.

Think of an interaction that left you feeling frustrated, angry, or upset. Use the chart below to ask yourself: What was the situation? What was the frustration? What was the feeling? What was the underlying need?

Situation: *I was with my friend Betty, and she interrupted my story to talk about her latest dating experience.*

WHAT WAS THE FRUSTRATION	WHAT WAS THE FEELING?	WHAT WAS THE UNDERLYING NEED?
I felt dismissed when she interrupted me while I was telling her something important.	Angry, hurt, unimportant	To feel understood, heard, valued, and important

Situation: _____

WHAT WAS THE FRUSTRATION	WHAT WAS THE FEELING?	WHAT WAS THE UNDERLYING NEED?

GET CLEAR WHERE A BOUNDARY IS NEEDED

You may already be clear on the boundary (or boundaries) you need to set.
If you haven't taken a resentment inventory yet, go to page 102 and take one
now. You can also check your Boundary Awareness Raising Tracker (page 54) for
boundaries you recorded to initiate or boundaries to enforce. This exercise will
help you gain clarity on all of the details for any situation in which you want or
need to set a boundary. This preparation is the foundation for constructing your
boundary scripts in the pages that follow.

Bring a situation to mind and answer the following questions:

➜ *Who do you need to set or maintain a boundary with and what is the*
relationship?

_____

_____

_____

➜ *What is the situation?*

_____

_____

_____

→ What is the underlying need?

_____

_____

_____

_____

→ What do you hope will happen?

_____

_____

_____

_____

_____

_____

Say It With Me 💬

I have the right to express and honor
all of my feelings if I so choose.

WRITING BASIC BOUNDARY SCRIPTS

Use the suggestions below to help you craft meaningful boundary scripts. The more you do it, the more natural it will become to assert your preferences, limits, and deal breakers. Practice does not necessarily make "perfect," but it does normalize the process of honoring and asserting your thoughts, feelings, and desires.

1. **Use "I" Statements.** Avoid using "you" statements that distance you from your feelings and imply blame. Instead, use statements that begin with "I would like . . ." Stay neutral and stick to one issue at a time.

2. **Take Responsibility for What You Want.** You do not need anyone's approval for what you want. Remember, this is your preference, desire, limit, or deal breaker you are talking about. As mentioned earlier in this section, be mindful to avoid adding qualifying statements to your requests (e.g., "You'll probably think this is crazy, but . . ."). Also, reduce approval-seeking questions (e.g., "Does that make sense?" "Is that okay?").

3. **Be Specific.** If you are seeking more time with your spouse, say, "I have a simple request that we make Tuesday nights our date night so we can spend more quality time together," not, "We never go out anymore. Would it kill you to make a plan?"(See how that is likely to NOT get you what you want?)

Use the sentence starters below and the information from the previous exercises to personalize and build your boundary script.

Sentence Starters

"I'd like to make a simple request . . ."

"I wanted to bring to your attention . . ."

"I wanted you to be aware of how I feel about . . .
and I'd appreciate it in the future if . . ."

"I thought you should know . . ."

"I needed to tell you . . ."

"I wanted to put it on your radar . . ."

"I want you to be aware of how I feel . . ."

"I've been noticing a pattern, and I wanted to talk about . . ."

"I wanted to talk to you about how I prefer to handle . . ."

Examples

SITUATION	BOUNDARY REQUEST
Your partner is late without letting you know.	"I'd like to make a simple request that you let me know if you are going to be more than ten minutes late so we don't ruin our evening by arguing."
SITUATION	**BOUNDARY REQUEST**
Your Uncle Bob wants to help you with your taxes. (You do not want or need his help.)	"I appreciate you wanting to help me with my taxes. If I need help, I will let you know."

➔ *Use the boxes below to bring to mind your own situation and practice constructing your own boundary request.*

SITUATION	BOUNDARY REQUEST
SITUATION	**BOUNDARY REQUEST**

SETTING BOUNDARIES WITH LIMITS

Negotiating for your boundaries is a skill. Sometimes your answer is a simple yes or no, and other times there are stipulations and limits you will need to express. Below are scenarios and examples of how to appropriately respond.

➔ *A friend asks you to help them with their garage sale on Saturday.*

Yes	Yes, I am happy to help.
No	I am committed to volunteering all day on Saturday so I'm sorry I can't help you.
With Limits	I'd love to help and am available between two and four in the afternoon.

➔ *A work colleague adds last-minute tasks for you to do on a shared project with a quick turnaround.*

Yes	Yes, I can hit that deadline for the added tasks.
No	I cannot take on these new tasks and hit the deadline as my plate is already full.
With Limits	I can do the tasks you've added if you extend the deadline by two days.

→ *At a family gathering, your cousin approaches, "I have been thinking about you and wondering why you and Bob split. Do you want to talk about it?"*

Yes	Yes, let's find a quiet corner to talk.
No	Thanks for your concern but I really don't feel like talking about it.
With Limits	I do want to talk about it but not here. Let's make a lunch date so we can talk privately.

Now You Try

We've included additional script starters for saying no and setting limits in the Sentence Starters & Quick Phrases in the back of the workbook starting on page 136.

→ *Your friends have planned a weekend away to an expensive resort. Normally you would go, and you want to spend time with them, but currently you need to save your money.*

Yes	
No	
With Limits	

➜ *Traditionally you host all of the family holidays and this year your family is expecting the same. You've decided you no longer want to host them all.*

Yes	
No	
With Limits	

➜ *Now you. Come up with a recent situation you encountered.*

_____

_____

_____

Yes	
No	
With Limits	

BOUNDARY BINGO

Let this be a fun and ongoing reminder of how good it feels to have healthy boundaries!

Be on the lookout for when you do any of the following things and mark them off the chart.

B	I	N	G	O
I negotiated for a preference instead of going with the flow.	I gently pointed out when someone was interrupting me.	I asked someone to listen with compassion instead of giving me advice.	I asked expansive questions instead of giving auto-advice.	I negotiated for what I wanted instead of just agreeing to what was offered.
I asked for help.	I set a boundary and did not take it back.	I asked for clarification instead of assuming.	I bought time instead of giving an insta-yes.	I said no when I wanted to say no.
I accepted help.	I planned out a boundary script.	FREEDOM	I refrained from gossiping.	I respected another's boundary.
I spoke up about a personal boundary situation.	I allowed myself to do something just for fun.	I gave myself permission to rest.	I didn't over-explain or justify my no.	I said yes when I wanted to say yes.
I used a sentence starter.	I set a boundary at work.	I set a boundary with a friend.	I set a boundary with a parent or sibling.	I didn't share personal information too soon.

CONSEQUENCES

Adding a consequence for a Repeat Boundary Offender is appropriate and advisable because without consequences for repeatedly violating a boundary, there's little motivation to change their behavior.

Effective boundary-setting includes a defined response when someone violates the agreed-upon boundary action. Creating and clearly stating consequences can motivate the other person to respect your boundaries, which, in turn, protects you and the relationship. The consequence will only be effective if it is meaningful to the other person, and you must be willing to follow through on the consequence you set.

SITUATION	ESTABLISHING A CONSEQUENCE
You have previously asked your partner to text you if they are going to be late for dinner.	"If you continue to be late for dinner without informing me, I will eat without you and put your food in the refrigerator."

Other examples of Repeat Offender consequence language options:

Situation: Your roommate keeps using your stuff without your permission.

Consequence: "If you use my things without my permission again, I'll lock them up so you can't access them."

Situation: Your friend keeps sharing your personal information without your permission.

Consequence: "If you share any more of my personal information without my permission, I'll stop sharing the intimate details of my life with you."

Situation: Your Uncle Bob keeps making racist or sexist comments.

Consequence: "If you make any more racist or sexist comments, I will end the conversation and leave the room."

Your Turn

➜ *Use the chart below to bring to mind your own situation and practice constructing your own boundary consequence.*

SITUATION	ESTABLISHING A CONSEQUENCE

Loving Reminder
Decisions motivated by fear of rejection or conflict
will rarely be in your best interest.

FOLLOWING THROUGH

Following through on your proposed consequences is a must and consistency is queen. Boundaries that are enforced only some of the time send mixed messages and eventually fail.

Keep in mind that the right boundaries and consequences for you to set are unique to you and your relationships. Understanding your action choices when you are experiencing repeated boundary violations can turn your frustration into empowerment. And you may make your boundary request once, and the other person may simply be grateful that you shared your preference and respect it on the first go-round. All relationships and tolerances are different.

Situation: You've already made a boundary request and followed up by informing them of a future consequence.

The person from the previous exercise was late to dinner without forewarning once again.

"If you continue to be late for dinner without informing me, I will eat without you and put your food in the refrigerator."

YOUR ACTION TO ENFORCE THE CONSEQUENCE	YOUR SCRIPT TO COMMUNICATE THE CONSEQUENCE
Put their food in the refrigerator and eat without them.	"Since you were late without letting me know again, I ate without you and put your food in the refrigerator. I'm upset that you are not keeping your word."

Your Turn

➔ *You set the following consequence with your college-aged child, and they spent over the agreed upon monthly budget again using the household credit card.*

Consequence:

> "If you cannot keep your word about your monthly spending, I will deactivate the credit card."

YOUR ACTION TO ENFORCE THE CONSEQUENCE	YOUR SCRIPT TO COMMUNICATE THE CONSEQUENCE

GET PROACTIVE

Preplanning your boundary interactions, when possible, is important for success. You'll craft different plans depending on the particular relationship, and whether or not you're dealing with a Boundary First-Timer or a Repeat Offender.

→ *Think about the specific boundary you are planning to set and take time to answer the questions below.*

Who is the person?

- What is your relationship and history with the person?
- What is the boundary you need to set with them?
- Where and when is the best time to approach them?
- What tone will you use?
- Is this a first-time request or are you dealing with a Repeat Offender?
- What specific words (script) will you use? Write out the specific words.

_____

_____

_____

_____

_____

_____

_____

_____

_____

_____

_____

_____

_____

_____

_____

_____

_____

_____

_____

→ *Once you have your script, say the words out loud in the mirror or role-play with a trusted friend to increase your confidence.*

VISUALIZE FOR SUCCESS

Visualization is a tried-and-true technique used by top-level athletes to enhance their performance outcomes. This psychological prep work creates the optimal conditions, internally and externally, to successfully make the boundary request. Since we only have control over ourselves, speaking up and clearly asserting our desired boundaries is the goal.

The other person's response will reveal what they are willing or capable of doing. For example:

If someone is unwilling to compromise, uninterested in the way you feel, or offended that you had the nerve to assert yourself, you will have the opportunity to respond appropriately and perhaps rethink the relationship.

A powerful aspect of creating what you want, whether a successful boundary request or anything else, is visualizing and feeling the feelings of having it. This involves using all of your senses while visualizing.

➡ *Start by thinking about a boundary conversation you want to initiate. Write a narrative of how you want the events to unfold (i.e., it's a beautiful day, you feel empowered, you fluidly articulate your truth, etc.).*

_____

_____

_____

_____

_____

_____

_____

_____

_____

_____

_____

Read the narrative back to yourself and feel the feelings of asserting your boundary easily. Conjure the feelings in your body and heart. Continue to read and feel the narrative daily up until the conversation. See and feel yourself being centered, calm, and content.

Go and Execute

Now, it's time to take action and go set the boundary!

Reminder: Exercising the courage to have a boundary conversation is a win regardless of how the other person reacts. Your healing and increased self-confidence comes from being able to assert your preferences, limits, and deal breakers.

Do It With Me 🙌

Take 5 minutes to do a loving-kindness meditation
to send good vibes to yourself and others.

BOUNDARY PUSHBACK

When you start setting boundaries, people are going to notice. Some will be grateful for the new instructions, and some won't. Don't let your decisions get derailed by your fear of the other person's response. This point is vital for your success.

It's crucial to understand that the other person's resistance or reaction is their side of the street, not yours. Being prepared for some pushback is prudent. You can handle it. Don't read their response (verbal or otherwise) as a signal to abort. Stay the course and have faith. Remember, change happens step by step. Just keep putting one foot in front of the other. One small shift at a time and your Boundary Boss training will pay off in your future happiness.

Remember, setting and maintaining healthy boundaries is not about rejecting or judging others, it's about taking care of you. When you change the boundary dances in your relationships, others may feel threatened and want to keep the status quo. Your job is to simply stick to your boundary.

Boundary Pushback Scenarios, Strategies, & Tips

→ *Your partner is upset because you can't take off work to travel for a holiday and wants you to go back to your boss to try to change their answer.*

STRATEGY	ACKNOWLEDGE THEIR FEELINGS AND STICK TO YOUR BOUNDARY.
Script	"I see you're upset, and I'm disappointed too, but I've already told you my request was denied, and I am not asking again. Can we please focus on making a plan to enjoy our time at home together?"

→ *Your aunt keeps trying to put meat on your plate ("A little bit of beef stroganoff never hurt anyone, and I worked so hard to make it just right!") even though you have been a vegetarian for a decade.*

STRATEGY	YOU CAN USE BODY LANGUAGE TO SUPPORT YOUR NO.
Script	(Hand up in the STOP position in front of your plate) "No, thanks, Aunt Betty." (no explanation needed), and if she tries again, take the exact same action.

In the examples below, construct your own boundary script variation in the space provided.

→ *When someone feels threatened by your growth. ("I don't even know who you are anymore with all your new 'boundary' talk!")*

Script	"I see you're upset and even though I am growing and learning, I am still the same person and I love you. I would love it if we could grow together."
Your Turn	

→ *Someone pressing you for inappropriate or intimate details.*

Script	"Why would you ask me that? Why would you want to know that? Thanks for your concern but I'm not into discussing this with you."
Your Turn	

➔ *Someone says you're overreacting.*

Script	"I am telling you how I feel, not asking for your opinion about my feelings. Can you please try to listen without being judgmental or defensive?"
Your Turn	

➔ *Someone laughing at or mocking you.*

Script	"Anytime you mock me or attempt to humiliate me, I will end the conversation. And if you continue to respond to my concerns that way, I will end our relationship."
Your Turn	

➔ *Addressing someone else's bad behavior.*

Script	"I understand that you were under pressure when you exploded the other night but that is not an excuse for screaming at me. I am happy to discuss how you're feeling when you're stressed but I am not willing to be an emotional punching bag. Do not let it happen again."
Your Turn	

➔ *Someone important to you dismissing your feelings/needs.*

Script	"You telling me I have 'no reason' to feel the way I do is not helpful. You don't need to approve of my feelings for them to be valid, but you DO need to care about the way I feel whether you understand it or not."
Your Turn	

Stay the course and have faith. Remember, change happens step by step. Just keep putting one foot in front of the other. One small shift at a time is how sustainable transformation is built!

Say It With Me 💬

I have the right to communicate my preferences, limits, and deal breakers.

ANALYZING A DISAPPOINTING BOUNDARY SITUATION

Starting to set boundaries can be anxiety-provoking, messy, and awkward. The more you do it, the better and easier it gets. If a boundary conversation doesn't go as planned, think about how you would have changed the interaction.

→ *Start by considering the following questions.*

YES	NO	
		Did I prepare for the conversation using script guidelines from this book before I approached the person?
		Did I choose the right time to ask or set the boundary?
		Was I clear in my request?
		Did I provide context or start with gratitude? (If needed, see 141)
		Should I have included a mutual agreement? (if appropriate, see 144)
		Should I have included a consequence? (if appropriate, see 111)
		Did I remain calm and neutral?
		Did I try to refrain from trying to "convince" them of my right to assert the boundary?
		Did my body language align with my feelings and my desired outcome?
		Was my tone appropriate?
		Did I practice what I was going to say ahead of time?

➔ *Based on your no answers, reflect and journal on what you would do differently next time.*

_____

_____

_____

_____

_____

_____

_____

_____

Now that you've mentally rehearsed and imprinted the process of revising the interaction, give yourself an opportunity to be courageous and consider revisiting the boundary conversation.

Do It With Me 🙌

Step outside for a 5-minute nature or walking break.

CELEBRATE BOUNDARY WINS

A mini-confetti party every time you choose your own empowerment? YES, YES, YES. Recognizing disordered boundary behavior and swiftly pivoting into new ones becomes easier and more natural the more you do it. Building a life aligned with your true heart's desires is so worth your effort.

➔ *In the space below, make a list of the first 5 boundaries you set! Especially the small ones since they are the foundation for your ultimate freedom. Also, share your boundary wins with a supportive pal or partner!*

SITUATION	BOUNDARY ACTION	RESULT
Betty ate my yogurt from the work refrigerator.	I made a simple request that she not eat food with my name on it.	She agreed to not eat my food in the future.

FOR YOUR BACK POCKET

Since you may not always have the time to preplan a boundary conversation, it's helpful to memorize and keep a couple of your fave scripts on hand so you always have the words you need.

→ *Fill in the blanks below with your favorite boundary starters from boundary examples given throughout the book and in the resource section. Once you have filled in the boxes, read these aloud often or even write them on Post-its and stick them to your mirror to help inspire you every day.*

REFLECT

This brings us to the end of our Go section of the workbook!

Please take a few minutes to reflect on what you learned in this phase of your Boundary Boss journey.

→ *What were your biggest Aha Moments?*

_____

_____

_____

_____

_____

→ *What were your biggest breakthroughs?*

_____

_____

_____

_____

_____

_____

_____

_____

_____

➜ *What did the exercises in this section bring up for you?*

_____

_____

_____

_____

_____

Say It With Me 💬

I have the right to talk true, be seen, and live free.

YOUR NEW BOUNDARY BASELINE

Woooo hoooo! You are almost at the finish line of your *Boundary Boss Workbook*! Please take ten minutes to revisit the Boundary Baseline questions (page 8) so you can see your progress!

→ *How would you describe your boundary status right now?*

_____

_____

_____

_____

_____

_____

_____

→ *How difficult do you find it to draw boundaries now? On a scale from 1 to 5, with 1 being easy and 5 being difficult:*

[1]　　[2]　　[3]　　[4]　　[5]
easiest　　　　　　　　　　　　　　　　very
　　　　　　　　　　　　　　　　　　　difficult

➜ *Does the thought of drawing boundaries create less anxiety for you now?*

☐ Yes ☐ No

➜ *Do you know what boundaries actually are and the importance of them?*

☐ Yes ☐ No

➜ *Do you use passive-aggressive communication to express your opinions when boundaries are being violated?*

☐ Yes ☐ No

➜ *Is your current anger, resentment, anxiety, fear, and/or frustration connected to boundary violations?*

☐ Yes ☐ No

➜ *Do you think people will view you as mean, selfish, rude, or offensive if you draw boundaries or speak up?*

☐ Yes ☐ No

➜ *Are you more confident setting boundaries with the following people now?*

☐ Spouse / Partner   ☐ Friends

☐ Children   ☐ Frenemies

☐ Parents   ☐ Boss

☐ Siblings   ☐ Coworkers

☐ Other Relatives   ☐ Other _____

☐ Lover / Date   ☐ Other _____

→ *Do you now know what is and is not okay for you?*

☐ Yes ☐ No

→ *List two to three of your biggest boundary desires you will be working on going forward.*

_____

_____

_____

_____

_____

_____

_____

_____

_____

_____

➜ *Now compare your answers.*

What has changed for you since you first did your Boundary Baseline assessment at the beginning of your *Boundary Boss Workbook* journey? Celebrate every win, every new thought, and every new action that you have taken throughout our time together. These are now the building blocks for your next-level boundaries and life as a Boundary Boss! Go, YOU!

_____

_____

_____

_____

_____

_____

_____

Loving Reminder 🩶

How you treat yourself sets the bar for every
other relationship in your life.

Parting Message

Congratulations, you did it! I hope that you are proud of yourself. (I know I am proud of you! 💕) Gentle reminder: transforming lifelong, ingrained boundary patterns takes practice and time, but it's the small, consistent changes that lead to the biggest breakthroughs and sustainable change. You got this, and I am here cheering you on!

Boundary Boss Workbook Resources

Here are additional boundary script writing resources for you that include: how to buy time instead of giving an insta-yes, additional script starters, how to say no with ease, and a section on techniques to make your boundary scripts more successful.

To further enhance your learning and make this workbook truly interactive, I have allocated space below each resource for you to make notes and write your own scripts. This is an opportunity for you to personalize the content and create boundary scripts that resonate with your unique circumstances.

Feel free to jot down any insights, ideas, or reflections that come to mind as you explore these resources. Use this space to craft boundary scripts that align with your preferences, desires, limits and deal breakers. Your personalized scripts will empower you to assert your boundaries confidently and effectively in various situations.

Remember, the act of writing down your thoughts and scripts can greatly reinforce your understanding and help you internalize the concepts. So, make the most of this dedicated space and make it your own.

I encourage you to engage with these resources actively, utilize the provided space, and create boundary scripts that truly reflect who you are and what you want to achieve. May this workbook be a catalyst for positive change and growth as you navigate the world of boundaries.

Happy scripting!

SENTENCE STARTERS & QUICK PHRASES:

"**I would like to make a simple request** that we take turns deciding where to meet for dinner."

"**I would really appreciate if you could** allow me to finish my story and then I am all ears for yours."

"**I would be more comfortable if** we could set a time to meet that works for both of us."

"**I thought you should know,** when you interrupt my story, it makes me feel unimportant or that you're not listening."

"**I wanted to bring this to your attention.** The last few times we've gotten together, I paid more than my share since I don't drink. I should have asked you not to include me in the bar tab at the time and will if it happens again."

"**I need to tell you that** telling Betty something I shared with you in confidence really bummed me out and broke my trust. Please don't do it again."

"**I want you to be aware of how I feel about** our interaction the other night."

"**I've noticed that** when I am talking, you are frequently on your phone. Can you please put it down so we can both be present and enjoy our time together."

STRATEGIES TO BUY TIME TO DECIDE:

"Thank you for asking. I will need to check my calendar and circle back."

"I will need to sleep on that. I have implemented a 24-hour decision-making policy."

"I want to check with (add name here) before committing."

"I will need to get back to you on that but thank you for thinking of me."

_____

_____

_____

_____

_____

_____

_____

_____

WAYS TO SAY NO:

"I appreciate the offer, but I don't think it's the right time for me."

"I appreciate the invitation, but I already have plans that day."

"I would love to join you, but unfortunately, I have a prior commitment."

"I'm honored that you asked, but I'm afraid I have to decline."

"I'm sorry, but I won't be able to make it. I hope you have a great time."

"Thanks for the invitation, but I'm not feeling up to it today."

"I would love to go, but I'm currently swamped with work."

_____

_____

_____

_____

_____

_____

CUSTOMIZING SCRIPTS:

Proactively customizing your boundary scripts to take into consideration the feelings of others can make your scripts even more successful. Sometimes it only takes a simple statement added to the beginning of a boundary request to diffuse a situation and increase the goodwill between you and another person. Positive reinforcement, acknowledgment of other people's emotions, and just being cordial increase the likelihood of a positive boundary interaction.

Start with Empathy

Emotional boundaries can be challenging to enforce, particularly with your VIPs. You can be sympathetic or empathetic to someone's situation without taking it on or going into "fix it" mode.

"Sounds like this has been an extremely difficult experience for you. I am witnessing you with so much compassion and am here to listen and support you" (giving support instead of advice).

_____

_____

_____

_____

_____

_____

Expressing Appreciation

> "I appreciate that you thought to include me but I have plans on Saturday already so will have to pass. I hope you have a great time!"

_____

_____

_____

_____

Expressing Gratitude

Recognition and gratitude are essential to the success of your boundary setting. The more goodwill, the more appreciated both people feel, the more flexible and durable the relationship becomes.

> "I appreciate you checking with me before committing to plans with Betty. Your consideration really makes me feel seen and loved. Thank you."

_____

_____

_____

Ask First

When it comes to respecting the boundaries of others, don't make assumptions. It can be tempting to think others are like us, but they may not be. By asking first you are creating space for the other person to safely share their boundary with you.

"Would it be okay if I gave you a hug? Looks like you could use some support right now."

"Is now a good time to chat?"

"Let me know when you have five minutes to talk through my presentation. I would really appreciate your input."

_____

_____

_____

_____

_____

_____

_____

_____

Time Management

It is not necessary or advisable to stop what you are doing the moment someone else makes a request. Being specific about when and if you can assist will manage all of the expectations and leave you with more bandwidth to prioritize what you need to do.

> "I'm caught up at the moment with something else, but I can meet with you at 4 pm today to go over your proposal."

_____

_____

_____

Saying No with Additional Context

Your deal breaker or nonnegotiable boundaries serve to protect you or someone else. Sometimes a simple but firm no works just fine. If you want to provide more clarity by adding context you can expand on your reasoning.

> "It's not personal, I just don't discuss my private life at work."

_____

_____

_____

Ending a Conversation

Healthy boundaries are part of maintaining good relationships, and they are also part of ending conversations when necessary.

> "This conversation is going nowhere and making me uncomfortable. I am hanging up now."

_____

_____

_____

_____

Adding a Mutual Benefit

Restating a boundary to include a mutual benefit for both parties is an effective way to ensure that the other person feels heard and respected while also addressing your own needs and values.

For the partner who is late without notice:

> "In the future, I'd like to make a simple request that if you are going to be more than fifteen minutes late, you let me know so I can keep the food hot (benefit) and we can avoid ruining our evening together by arguing (benefit)."

For the person that borrows your stuff without asking:

"I'd like to make a simple request that in the future, if you would like to borrow something of mine that you ask me first, so we can continue to share our clothes (benefit) and avoid ruining our weekly sister time by arguing (benefit)."

For the pal who calls you at 11 pm:

"I appreciate our conversations but 11 is too late for me. How about we schedule our calls during the day, so I can be fully present (benefit) and we can both get the emotional support we need (benefit)?"

_____

_____

_____

_____

_____

_____

_____

_____

Getting a Verbal Agreement

If you have already verbally set a boundary with someone and they still break the boundary, it can be impactful to make your boundary request with a mutual benefit attached.

"So can we agree that if I cook, you will clean up the kitchen?"

_____

_____

_____

_____

_____

_____

_____

_____

_____

To Go Back to a Past Situation

For some reason, many of us believe there is a statute of limitations when it comes to addressing past grievances. I say, not true. It is never too late to attempt to be seen and heard or to honor your experiences. Remember, it's best to keep things simple and straightforward.

"You know, I've been thinking about an interaction we had last month/last year/ in the summer of '78, and I'd like to share my thoughts and feelings about that . . ."

"I was reflecting on something that happened last week, and it would be meaningful for me to share with you that . . ."

"Look, I wish I had said something when this happened, but it's bothering me now, so I want to bring it to your attention . . ."

_____

_____

_____

_____

_____

_____

SCENARIOS:

For Friends Who Attempt to Initiate Gossip

"Honestly, I'd much rather talk about YOU and your new project/apartment/relationship."

"I am officially on a negativity cleanse so no gossip for me, it really brings me down."

"Please tell me we have better things to yak about than Betty and her boyfriend issues!"

_____

_____

_____

_____

_____

_____

_____

When Confiding in a Spontaneous Advice-Giver

"I have a situation I want to share with you and I am not seeking advice or your opinion at the moment. Can you just listen with compassion please?"

"I want to share what is going on for me and ask that you simply listen with compassion without offering advice or criticism. I would really appreciate that."

_____

_____

_____

_____

_____

_____

_____

_____

_____

When Someone Attempts to Talk You Out of Your No

"You asked, and I've answered."

"No, thank you. My decision is made and I'm asking you to respect it."

_____

_____

_____

_____

_____

_____

_____

_____

_____

_____

Someone Who Tries to Blame You

"Instead of blaming, let's please discuss."

"I feel your pain, but I don't think I am the correct recipient of your anger. I am not willing to take the blame for this situation."

_____

_____

_____

_____

_____

_____

_____

_____

_____

_____

Jealous or Bossy Friends

"I'm sorry you feel hurt. I love you, and I have other friends that are also important to me. Please don't expect to be included in every one of my plans."

"Please stop trying to control me with guilt."

"I'd love it if you would simply be happy for me."

_____

_____

_____

_____

_____

_____

_____

_____

_____

Someone Who Negates Your Feelings

When you have expressed your feelings, and someone replies, "You shouldn't feel that way," "That's ridiculous," or "No you don't," you can say:

"That is not helpful. I'd appreciate it if you would simply care that I am upset."

"I'm telling you how I feel, not asking for your opinion on my feelings."

_____

_____

_____

_____

_____

_____

_____

_____

_____

_____

Challenges to Your Deal Breaker

"This is nonnegotiable."

"I'm not seeking your approval or opinion about my feelings/preferences/deal breakers. I am simply informing you of them."

_____

_____

_____

_____

_____

_____

_____

_____

_____

To Share Something Important

For an auto-advice giver or interrupter: "I have something important I would like to share with you. Can you please let me finish my thoughts before interjecting yours? I promise to do the same for you so that we may both feel fully understood."

If you get tongue-tied when sharing: "I have written down a few things that I want to communicate to you, so can you please wait until I am done sharing them with you before responding? You know that asking for what I want is challenging for me and I would really appreciate your patience and compassion while I work to get better at it."

_____

_____

_____

_____

_____

_____

_____

_____

_____

_____

_____

_____

_____

_____

_____

_____

_____

_____

_____

Say It With Me 💬

I have the right to make mistakes,
course correct, or change my mind.

Acknowledgments

It takes a village to write a book! I want to extend a deep bow of gratitude to those who have made this project possible.

Thank you to . . .

Tracey Charlebois, for tirelessly helping flesh out the content of this workbook and making it a reality.

Joyce Juhasz, for your stellar organizational skills and always being the last eyes on everything.

The editors and staff at Sounds True, for their professionalism, support, and commitment to mental health.

My hubs, Victor, for his flexibility and unending love and support.

Finally, I want to thank every single person who will engage with this workbook. Your dedication to your own growth and mental wellness will create a powerful, positive ripple effect that the world desperately needs. Thank you.

About the Author

Terri Cole is a licensed psychotherapist and relationship expert based in New York. She is the author of *Boundary Boss: The Essential Guide to Talk True, Be Seen, and (Finally) Live Free* and the founder of several programs, including Real Love Revolution, Boundary Bootcamp, and Crushing Codependency.

Before becoming an expert in love, boundaries, and codependency, Terri spent years as a bicoastal talent agent negotiating endorsement contracts for supermodels and celebrities. However, her eventual disenchantment with the world of entertainment led her to make a career change in her thirties and become a psychotherapist and empowerment expert. Her mission has been to help women lead self-determined lives that they love by teaching them how to establish and maintain healthy boundaries with ease and create and sustain vibrant relationships.

Over the past two decades, Terri has worked with a wide range of individuals, including international pop stars, athletes, Broadway performers, TV personalities, thought leaders, and Fortune 500 CEOs. She empowers a global community of over 800,000 individuals across 189 countries each week through her illuminating videos, articles and blog posts, therapeutic meditations, online courses, and popular podcast The Terri Cole Show.

Terri's approach integrates practical psychology with Eastern mindfulness practices, resulting in a unique blend that allows her to simplify complex psychological concepts for her clients and students. Her gift lies in making these concepts not only accessible but also actionable, leading to sustainable change.

Recognized as an expert therapist and master life coach, she has appeared on popular shows such as *GMA3*, *The Doctors*, and *NBC News Daily*, as well as being featured on the *Real Housewives* and hundreds of podcasts. She is a contributor to major publications, including *The Huffington Post*, *Well+Good*, *Oprah Daily*, and *Shondaland*, and has been highlighted in *People* magazine, *The New York Times*, *Women's Day*, *Glamour*, *Elle*, *Forbes*, *Vogue*, *Cosmopolitan*, *CNN*, and *Self*. Learn more about her work at terricole.com.

About Sounds True

Sounds True was founded in 1985 by Tami Simon with a clear mission: to disseminate spiritual wisdom. Since starting out as a project with one woman and her tape recorder, we have grown into a multimedia publishing company with a catalog of more than 3,000 titles by some of the leading teachers and visionaries of our time, and an ever-expanding family of beloved customers from across the world.

In more than three decades of evolution, Sounds True has maintained our focus on our overriding purpose and mission: to wake up the world. We offer books, audio programs, online learning experiences, and in-person events to support your personal growth and awakening, and to unlock our greatest human capacities to love and serve.

At SoundsTrue.com you'll find a wealth of resources to enrich your journey, including our weekly *Insights at the Edge* podcast, free downloads, and information about our nonprofit Sounds True Foundation, where we strive to remove financial barriers to the materials we publish through scholarships and donations worldwide.

To learn more, please visit SoundsTrue.com/freegifts or call us toll-free at 800.333.9185.

Together, we can wake up the world.